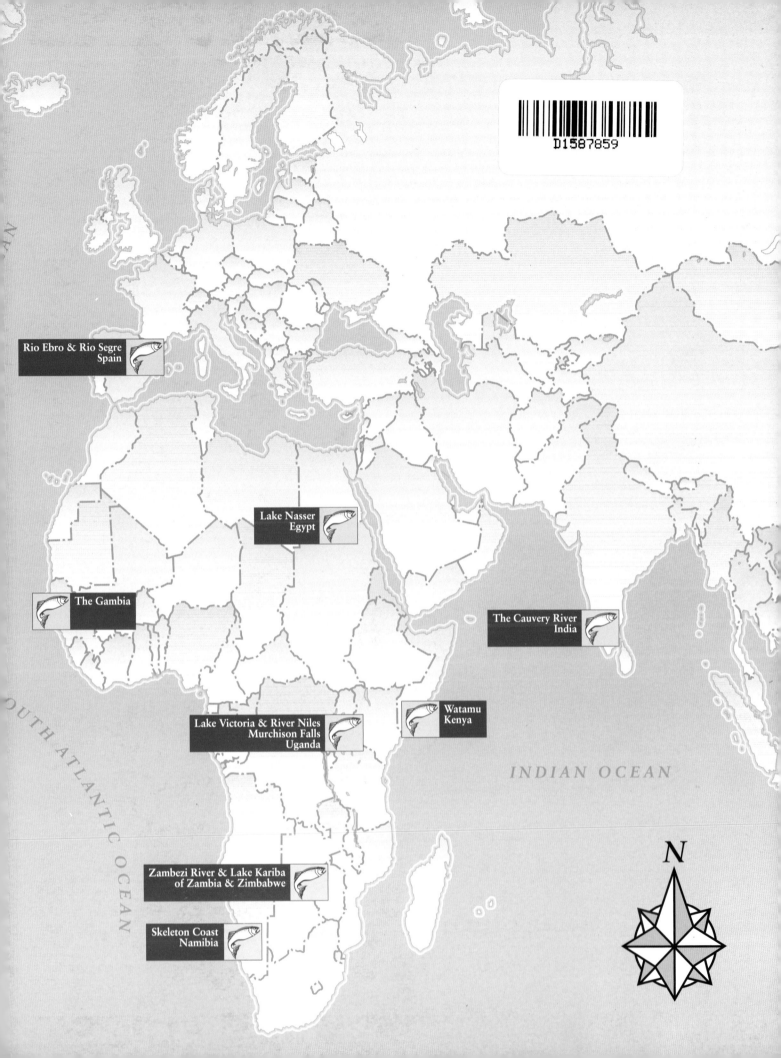

Rio Ebro & Rio Segre
Spain

Lake Nasser
Egypt

The Gambia

The Cauvery River
India

Lake Victoria & River Niles
Murchison Falls
Uganda

Watamu
Kenya

INDIAN OCEAN

Zambezi River & Lake Kariba
of Zambia & Zimbabwe

Skeleton Coast
Namibia

SOUTH ATLANTIC OCEAN

N

JOHN WILSON'S
GREATEST FISHING
ADVENTURES

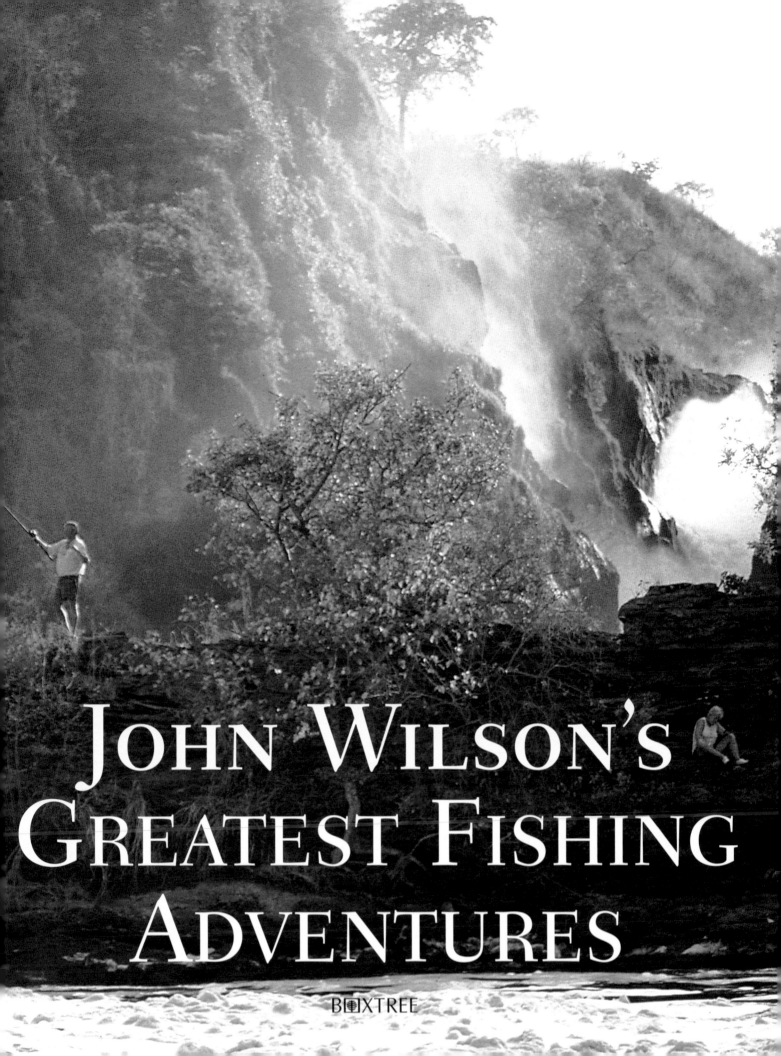

JOHN WILSON'S
GREATEST FISHING
ADVENTURES

BOXTREE

For Margaret Emily Wilson and Denis Sydney Wilson, my dear parents,
who both sadly passed away before their eighty-ninth birthdays in 2001.
Never short of encouraging words, particularly during my childhood,
they were forever reminding me to live life to the full. I miss them terribly
and dedicate this volume to their memory.

Previous page *John fishes the white water immediately below the Devil's Cauldron on the River Nile at Murchison Falls for the legendary Nile perch and big catfish. Three species in this river grow to weights in excess of 100lb.*

First published 2002 by Boxtree
an imprint of Pan Macmillan Ltd
Pan Macmillan, 20 New Wharf Road, London N1 9RR
Basingstoke and Oxford
Associated companies throughout the world
www.panmacmillan.com

ISBN 0 7522 1969 3

3 5 7 9 8 6 4

A CIP catalogue record for this book is available from
the British Library.

Design by Dan Newman/Perfect Bound Ltd
Colour Reproduction by Aylesbury Studios Ltd
Printed by Butler & Tanner Ltd, Frome and London

CONTENTS

Acknowledgements

In addition to the debt I owe my ever-tolerant wife and soulmate, Jo, bless her, for encouraging me to pursue each new interest within angling knowing full well it will ultimately mean I spend more time overseas, I would also like to thank fellow anglers who have added value to what you are about to view and read – friends such as Walt Jennings from Florida, Stu McKay from Winnipeg, Paul Goldring from Entebbe, Marco Magyar from Kampala, Mark Longster from Banjul, Susheel Gyanchand from Bangalore, Fred Helman from Chilliwack in British Columbia, plus Andy Davison, Christine Slater, Andy Hardy, Don Metcalfe, Jim Tyree, Peter Coleshaw, Simon Clarke, Keith Lambert, Gary Allen, Carl Pashley, David Lewis and Stewart Smalley. Finally I would like to acknowledge the wonderful contribution of my typist, Jan Carver, in bringing this book into being.

INTRODUCTION

The Oxford dictionary defines the word safari as 'an overland expedition especially in Africa'. I, however, have taken the liberty of expanding that meaning so I can take the reader on safari not only through the vast continent of Africa, but beyond, to some of the world's most exciting and awesome locations – over land and by air, and also by river and by sea, to a total of 14 destinations where numerous exotic species topping 100lb can be caught. Where space has permitted I have given a résumé of the techniques, tackle and baits required, although it is my intention that this volume be more evocative and inspirational than 'how to' in nature.

As a freelance angling journalist, who also escorts parties of anglers to foreign destinations, I have been most fortunate for over a decade now in sampling exotic sportsfishing all over the world. But I am not alone. In these days of global mobility, travelling far afield to do battle with some of the most thrilling adversaries in both salt- and freshwater, is fortunately now within everyone's reach. According to the international passenger survey instigated by the Office of National Statistics way back in 1968, for instance, slightly fewer than five million trips were made abroad by Britons. A decade later in 1978 the figure had risen to almost eight million. In 1988 it had escalated to over 20 million and in 1998 a massive 32 million overseas trips were made.

The exhilarating, acrobatic and legendary species featured in the following pages include gladiators like mahseer, sailfish, tarpon, Wels catfish, bronze whaler sharks, tiger fish, amberjacks, bonefish, channel catfish, Nile perch, vundu catfish, chinook salmon, white sturgeon and many others. They may not be everyone's choice amongst the world's greatest battlers, but they happen to be mine.

John Wilson
Great Witchingham, 2002

LAKE NASSER
EGYPT

Enthusiastic water gardeners will no doubt already be aware that in ancient Egypt coloured water lilies were cultivated as far back as the XIIth Dynasty, some 3,000 years before Christ. Such is the history and mystery of this the Land of the Pharaohs, so incredibly rich in perfumes, gold, silver and silks, where its temples, pyramids and the civilized world's oldest monarchies help to make Egypt arguably the most fascinating country within the vast continent of Africa. And when the life blood of Egypt, the mighty Nile, became flooded all the way south to the Sudan following the construction of the high dam at Aswan in the 1960s, thus creating massive Lake Nasser, little did travelling freshwater anglers know what fabulous sportsfishing the future would hold.

Indigenous species of the Nile, such as vundu and bagrus catfish, tiger fish, the legendary Nile perch, tilapia (the staple food fish of Africa), plus numerous multicoloured and strange species such as electric catfish (capable of emitting pulses of over 300 volts) and the parrot-beaked puffer fish, soon spread and reproduced in their new environment. It is perhaps worth noting at this point that Nile tiger fish, though occasionally caught into double figures, do not reach the heavy weights of those in the Zambezi River. Nasser tigers are noticeably thinner and exceptionally long for their average weight of around 3-6lb. They can, however, provide great sport on both light spinning and fly-fishing outfits, particularly from the shore.

As a flooded desert, Lake Nasser is a unique sheet of water covering some 300 miles in length and varying between 5 and over 20 miles across, with countless islands and numerous khors (once valleys) along its eastern shoreline, providing a wealth of fishing hot spots around which to troll or go ashore to work a lure parallel to the rocky bank. This is a hot (temperatures topping 100 degrees Fahrenheit at midday) and mystical environment where trees as such do not exist. There are simply squat bushes and grasses along parts of the shoreline only, where jackals, desert foxes and gerbils live. Add scorpions, snakes, lizards and the most monstrous monitors along the rockiest parts of the shoreline and island tops, plus the occasional huge Nile crocodile and you have just some of the creatures of the lake. The bird life is simply phenomenal too with all kinds of waders including flamingos, plus pelicans, egrets, geese, Goliath herons, and several

Previous spread *This is the awesome magnitude of* Lates niloticus, *the legendary Nile perch. To display this superb hundred and thirty-four pounder, just one of four buffaloes (specimens over 100lb) I caught in a week's trolling, I needed the help of Lake Nasser guide Mohamed.*

Above *What a spectacle for the eyes of visiting anglers. Built by Rameses II to impose fear upon the Nubians, these ancient statues of the pharaohs fronting the temples at Abu Simbel on the lake's western shoreline were actually transported from lower down the valley when the River Nile was flooded and a high dam constructed at Aswan to create Lake Nasser.*

birds of prey, including buzzards, ospreys, Egyptian vultures, kites, eagles and owls. For such an enigmatic, seemingly harsh and bare environment, Lake Nasser is so incredibly productive. Occasionally you are treated to a glimpse of donkeys, camels or goats along the shoreline, animals of the wandering desert tribesmen who prove that a living can be earned from sand, rock and sun.

For those equally interested in the history of the Nile, halfway down the lake at Abu Simbel stand the majestic statues carved in rock of the pharaohs, built by Ramses II to instil fear among the Nubians. Visitors, incidentally, have the choice of starting their safari from Abu Simbel and working the southern end down to the Sudanese border, or boating down the northern end of the lake from Aswan. There are regular flights between these two points.

Nasser has a rocky and sandy, often mountainous shoreline, the most habitat-rich areas being around the tops of hills (now islands) and sunken rocky plateaux where the perch lie in wait beside boulders and in caverns into which a car would fit. Along both the shoreline and around the islands, look for sheer-sided cliff faces where the rock is broken providing overhangs and prime ambush points, and you will have located a potential Nile perch hot spot. Whilst trolling close to sheer-sided rock faces for instance, just 10 to 20 feet out, it is not uncommon for the fish finder/sonar unit to be reading over 100 feet of water beneath the boat. Depths through the lake's central channel incidentally shelve down to in excess of 300 feet. To say that Lake Nasser offers a totally

wild, challenging, even dangerous form of safari-style fishing is an understatement. This is 'heart-in-your-mouth' stuff. Fighting one of the largest freshwater fish on this planet on stepped-up carp gear or a multiplier–uptide rod outfit (the perfect combo for trolling), results in savage takes and a powerful, uncompromising, deep-down, dogged fight, culminating in several gill-flaring, tail-walking leaps or lunges across the surface usually at the end of the fight (which is when the lure is often shaken out) before the perch is ready for unhooking. Your prize may well be so large that it cannot be held up for the camera by one man alone.

The attraction, of course, is that few British anglers have ever seen a freshwater fish in excess of that magical 100lb figure. Fewer still have successfully fought and landed one and been privileged to hold one up to be photographed. We are talking world-wide here of course, because where else (save for river-hooked Wels catfish) can you fish from the shore and stand a chance of hooking into not just a 100lb perch, but monsters of 200lb plus. But even these are nothing compared to the 375lb giant caught on a commercial long line. Just about every week of the year (except between June and August when, due to extreme heat, the lake is rested), 100lb-plus Nile perch are caught from the six trolling boats operated with local Nubian crews by Kenyan-born Tim Baily, better known as the African Angler.

Actually my own experiences with this fascinating gladiator first started on Lake Victoria (featured in Chapter 12) in the early 1990s when, in the company of Andy

Left *My long-time fishing buddy Andy Davison relies upon the inherent stretch in his 30lb monofilament reel line whilst applying maximum pressure to a powerful adversary, hell bent on diving beneath the boat. Andy won and the perch weighed 137lb.*

Below left *To tempt, play, land and unhook one of the planet's largest freshwater fish, the visiting angler requires some serious equipment. A comprehensive selection of sturdy, deep-diving plugs and replacement trebles is mandatory, plus bolt croppers, long-nosed pliers and a hand file.*

Below *Wandering the ancient back-streets of Aswan to haggle over the price of gold or spices is just one fascinating part of an angling safari on Lake Nasser.*

Davison and the *Go Fishing* television crew, I made a half-hour programme about trolling for Nile perch out of Rusinga Island which is on the Kenyan border of the lake. Ironically this very programme, when seen by Tim Baily, encouraged him to explore other African lakes for Nile perch and eventually led him to Aswan in Egypt and Lake Nasser. It is a series of events which inevitably draws Andy, Tim and I close together as friends but rarely do we all three fish together. So we decided to join up in December 1999 for a week's safari on Lake Nasser, specifically concentrating upon new areas and not the guaranteed hot spots where we had taken guests in the past. What a memorable safari it was, with my favourite guide, Mohamed, steering the 25-foot trolling boat and a 30-foot supply boat in attendance meeting up at various islands or parts of the shoreline each evening for meals and drinks. The lake then was at the highest level it had ever been since the high dam was constructed – the water level was over 20 feet higher than when I had last fished there in May.

Normally the most reliable features along which to troll and shore-fish for Nile perch are those veritable walls of rock (the tops of flooded hills of course) and around rocky promontories where perch characteristically lie in wait for a shoal of tilapia (their staple diet) or a group of tiger fish, or alestes (herring-like fish) or even a small- to medium-sized Nile perch. Nile perch are wonderful ambush artists and while they readily chase a lure, generally they'll lose interest after a few yards.

During the warmer months, from March to June, visitors generally catch far more perch – fish in the 10-40lb range being par for the course – particularly when shore-fishing. I can vividly remember a particular afternoon when working an orange Rapala CD14 plug (my favourite shore lure) up from the lake bed 30 feet down from the sheer-sided wall at Khor Maria, along Nasser's eastern shoreline, when I hooked a perch of around 15lb that simply went berserk. It even jumped completely clear of the surface by several feet. Then as it neared the rocky shore I could see why. A couple of feet below looking up at its next meal was a monstrous Nile perch, fully 6 feet long, 2 feet deep and around 20 inches thick. I had been trolling for marlin off Madeira that same year and caught a 220lb big-eyed tuna, so I knew what two hundredweight of meat looked like. The perch dwarfed it. It was truly awesome. Part of my brain hoped it didn't take the hooked perch, because on an 18lb reel line, small multiplier and 11-foot stepped-up carp rod (standard shore gear) frankly I was out of my depth. But something inside also reminded me that one of the trebles on the small plug in the hooked perch was dangling free. Then the giant slowly sank down again and despite my continuing to throw just about every lure in my armoury through the same area for the following hour I never saw that monster again – and haven't since.

Whilst shore-fishing in deep water I find that sinking/diving artificials such as the Rapala CD14 which can be counted down (at around one foot per second) to the desired depth work best. Along relatively shallow shorelines however the Rapala Super Shad Rap floating diver, which descends to around 6-8 feet, is excellent and will usually float up to the surface when caught in rocks if slack line is given.

Left *Another 'buffalo' for Andy. Note its huge tail, supported by African Angler Tim Baily, and the equally massive reinforced weigh sling, specially manufactured for us by Wychwood Tackle. Perch are guided into the protective sling in the water, then hoisted on board (it takes two) and onto the scales.*

Right *Note the huge swallow-like tail, mother-in-law dentistry and incredible length of this double-figure tiger fish. Compared to those of the Zambezi system (see page 114) on a weight for length basis, Lake Nasser tigers are considerably slimmer and consequently weigh nowhere near so heavy.*

Next spread *This monster from the deeps (actually it grabbed an orange CD18 Rapala trolled in only twenty feet of water) weighing 162lb and caught by my guide, Mohamed, on Tim's rod while he was taking a turn steering the boat, is one of the most superbly proportioned specimens of the species it has ever been my privilege to photograph. Was Mohamed over the moon or what? Even Tim is smiling. The perch was in fact our largest of no less than ten buffaloes caught in just one week's trolling. Lake Nasser has few equals.*

Historically far fewer perch but much larger individual specimens are caught from mid-October through to Christmas as the Egyptian winter settles in. The coldest months are January and February. Then during the latter part of March temperatures start to rise again and summer fishing begins. Prior to the trip in question I could not understand why larger perch were caught during the winter but I am now certain it has much to do with their spawning cycle.

As I have already mentioned, we were looking for new ground. We chose a depth band of between 15 and 30 feet, much of which would consist of virgin, recently flooded lake bed. The largest concentrations of adult perch were, without question, around clusters of boulders and dense weed beds in depths averaging around 20–25 feet. A common denominator was that these now sunken islands, plateaux and ridges of rock that anglers had been shore-fishing from just a few months earlier, had on one side

the deep water of the open lake and on the other vast areas of weedy shallows where the tilapia feed close to the shore. It goes without saying here that constant viewing of the sonar screen was imperative.

Drawing upon my knowledge of perch in British stillwaters which require a medium upon which to drape their eggs, either sunken branches or dense weed beds, I deduced that perhaps here were areas occupied by big female Nile perch only, as perhaps an early grouping process prior to their eventual spawning later in January and February. The smaller males were totally conspicuous by their absence and I wasn't surprised. A big female can easily gulp down a 20-pounder without batting an eyelid, and until their actual courtship rituals begin they would of course be fair game. What also added weight to my theory was that in the two separate areas which eventually produced all the whoppers, though some 50 miles apart, the very same long and slender-leaved, curly pond weed (very similar to our own *Potamogeton crispus* but with more elongated, distinctly pointed leaves on long stalks) was sprouting in dense beds several feet above the bottom. The perfect spawning medium perhaps?

Late one afternoon we located some large perch on the sonar situated over weed-covered, boulder-strewn sunken islands. We decided to give the entire area (a good 100 acres or so of similar habitat) a thorough search the following morning from first light and return to the supply boat after a couple of hours for breakfast. But we experienced such unbelievable action no one even mentioned breakfast. It started with some slamming takes from tiger fish in the half-light as we trolled Rapala Shad Raps over the shallows on our way out from a small island where we had tied up for the night, heading for the huge area of sunken islands. But as always most managed to shed the hooks, though we boated two of around 6lb apiece.

We then changed over to deep divers as Mohamed, our guide, slowly tacked the boat over a consistent depth averaging between 20 and 30 feet where every so often the Humminbird fish finder bleeped as it marked small groups of what we took to be big perch lying amongst the mixture of huge boulders and dense weed beds. Anticipation was at a high level. Andy was first away as a perch of around 80lb grabbed his gold Russelure, jumped twice and promptly shot beneath the boat to wrap the 30lb reel line around the propeller. This necessitated unravelling other bits of line and actually taking the propeller off, during which time we drifted over shallower water and when Mohamed restarted the engine the finder read just 16 feet. I swung my plug out anyway, a Reef Digger, and almost expected it to weed up but it never stood a chance. Within seconds of putting the 10000 multiplier into gear, over went my Voyager rod into a pulsating full curve and away shot a very big fish, ripping line fast from a firmly set clutch. After about 60 yards it shot to the surface in one of those classic gill-flaring Nile perch lunges and shook its head angrily whilst trying to tail walk. That's the beauty of this awesome species, you are treated to spectacular tail-walking action during the closing stages of every battle following deep-down, dogged fights, though some fish will repeatedly surface from the minute they feel the hooks go in, in an effort to shake the plug out. This was one such fish and it was a monster, a buffalo for certain. All perch over 100lb incidentally are called buffaloes by Nasser regulars because of their distinctly humped backs. Lovely.

Above *This is the most spectacular yet worrying moment of any battle with a big Nile perch, when it rushes up to the surface and jumps, Polaris style, its huge mouth wide open, in a gill-flaring acrobatic display of pure aggression, trying to rid itself of your artificial. Indeed, at no time during the encounter are those hooks more likely to be shaken out and I'm sure many a seasoned Nile perch enthusiast, myself included, can attribute lost monsters to such occasions. Fortunately for Andy this whopper stayed on.*

Below *Consider the readout on the fish-finder screen. While my rod tip is almost touching the huge slabs of overhanging rock at the top of what was once a steep-sided hill, over sixty feet of water lies beneath the boat. Such are the wild and rugged sub-surface secret feature lies available to the Nile perch of Lake Nasser. And around each and every island you troll or shore-fish, the depth and rock formations are entirely different.*

Fortunately the trebles stayed in and within ten minutes I eased the monster towards Mohamed who had a hand gaff at the ready. You may wonder about the ethics of holding the perch steady on the gaff with its head above water whilst extracting the size 5/0 trebles. The Nile perch is an awesomely strong creature with sharp edges to its gill plates and sharp spines on its dorsal fin, the thickness of 6-inch nails. It's certainly not the kind of creature to handle flippantly. The method is far kinder to both the perch and the person unhooking it. Netting is completely out of the question and the spectacle of a large treble connected to both angler and a thrashing perch is not very palatable – I've seen it several times. This is one reason why I had my good friend, Stainless-steel Steve of Lymington make up a batch of hand gaffs, 14 inches long in 8mm stainless steel with T-bar handles, so your hand is well away from the trebles whenever the perch shakes its head, and they have proved so efficient. Such a tiny slit in the perch's soft skin immediately under its chin is actually less visible afterwards than hook marks. The perch weighed 134lb, at that moment my largest ever, beating my previous best by some 14lb. What a start!

Naturally I was over the moon and after taking some trophy shots we soon had three rods out trolling again. Andy quickly followed suit in a blazing red-hot spell with specimens of 55lb and 92lb before hitting the jackpot with a monster of 137lb. I then connected with another obvious buffalo as I saw getting on for 80–100 yards of 35lb line leave the reel against a firm clutch before the hooks suddenly and inexplicably dropped out. In fact they came back as if they had been bent with a pair of pliers. How Nile perch accomplish such destruction of size 5/0 cadmium-plated, extra-strong trebles within a matter of seconds has always amazed me. This is one reason why the weak bronze hooks on certain large lures are immediately replaced by plated, extra-strong trebles before use. We also sometimes either remove the middle hook (of three-hook plugs) or the one nearest the head. If too many hooks find purchase in the perch's huge expandable mouth (a 100-pounder could swallow a football) when it opens wide to head shake, leverage from the plug itself could end up ripping them all out.

Shortly after commencing trolling again I accounted for an 84-pounder whilst Andy took a mere baby of 35lb. These were all deep-bellied females and came to a mixture of artificials: Russelures, Reef Diggers and Rapala CD18s attached to our 4-foot long 100lb test mono traces. Wire incidentally dampens the lure's action dramatically and is simply not necessary even for huge perch. Once the 100lb mono becomes scuffed by the two abrasive pads (full of tiny teeth) situated inside both the top and bottom jaw, it is instantly replaced.

Tim, who had pulled free from a couple of good perch but until now had brought nothing to the boat, handed his rod over to Mohamed while he took the engine to search around. Mohamed had been holding Tim's rod for less than a couple of minutes when over it went and, though he didn't know it at the time, Mohamed was connected to his largest perch ever which led him a real song and dance, exploding almost completely clear of the surface on several occasions. Even Tim could not begrudge Mohamed such a fine fish. As a guide he rarely fishes because he is always on the engine or unhooking monsters hooked by guests. We were all totally ecstatic when his buffalo was finally played out, unhooked and hoisted in the weigh sling on to the scales. At 162lb it was the largest of the week.

Finally in the early afternoon when all action ceased we returned to the supply boat for our long-awaited breakfast, thinking we'd just experienced our best day's perch fishing ever. How wrong can you be? Strangely the evening session produced little other than a tiger fish – obviously active when the big perch were not. There isn't a tiger fish in the lake (and they grow to 15lb plus) which cannot be swallowed by a 50lb perch, remember. Likewise the following morning the perch were inactive as we worked our lures over the very same sunken islands from a dawn start. But once the full force of the sun finally illuminated everything down below to a certain level – and don't ask me what, because it was as though someone had flicked a switch – those big old female perch suddenly became unbelievably aggressive. But they were only interested in colourful lures trolled much higher above the bottom structure than the previous day – they wanted a chase. The killing patterns were, without question, double-jointed floating/diving-depth raiders in the bright Fire Tiger colour and Nilsmater Invincible in Nubian Sunset. An erratic, faster zigzag trolling route with the lure a good 50 yards behind the boat also accounted for many more hits.

Trolling is never simply a matter of towing a lure behind the boat and relying upon a mixture of patience and Lady Luck as many believe. Changing lures regularly to patterns of varying actions, colours and diving capabilities is very much order of the day, plus constantly retrieving to remove particles of weed which might impair both the action and the predator's inclination to grab hold of a particular artificial. Add to this trolling speed and the distance you pay out each lure behind the boat and you have an enormous number of variables. That's why it's so exciting. Generally speaking our three lures would be out somewhere between 25 and 40 yards but distances of up to 60 yards are sometimes required to induce takes, particularly in really clear water.

Andy belted into a whole string of monsters which ended up with a 139-pounder, his best of the week. Tim was unbelievably unfortunate with several klonkers slipping the hooks, and actually boated just one of around 40lb. Like Andy I also just couldn't go wrong and achieved buffaloes of 121lb and 141lb, my largest ever, plus a baby of 24lb, a 40-pounder and another of 81lb. It was difficult to remember a day when we have boated so many monsters (in either fresh- or saltwater) in such a comparatively short time. Certainly landing four over 100lb in one session will be a difficult act to beat. (But when you think about the ever-increasing potential of Lake Nasser, I am tempted to have a go. During the period from 16 September 1998 to 15 January 1999 Tim's six boats produced a staggering 66 perch of over 100lb for anglers from all around the world.)

As usual a certain percentage of fish hooked managed to come adrift, but that's lure fishing and you have to look philosophically even at obvious buffaloes which on their first or second lunge across the surface spit the plug straight back at you. Strangely even in comparatively shallow depths (most fish were hooked in less than 20 feet of water), we still had problems with a few perch 'blowing' or 'gassing-up' where a build-up of excess air in their swim bladders prevents their immediate return to the depth at which they were holding. This is a problem solved by lowering the perch down to the

Right Watched by African Angler and good friend Tim Baily (top right of pic), who pioneered this unique and marvellous safari-style fishing on Lake Nasser, my nephew Richard Wilson works a deep-diving plug close beside a vertical rock face along the lake's eastern shoreline. Here in the depths, which shelve to fifty feet, perch lie in wait amongst overhanging rocks ready to ambush passing shoals of tilapia or tiger fish. There are few more evocative, dangerous and productive locations than this anywhere in the world, where hooking into freshwater leviathans of up to and even over 200lb from the shore is a genuine reality.

bottom on the anchor rope (attached with fine cord threaded to form a loop either through the mouth and gills or a gaffing slit) and leaving it for half an hour connected to a marker buoy. Or, the perch is simply lowered down to the bottom with a heavy weight attached to a slip knot and the knot pulled before retrieving both weight and cord. This is by far the easiest and quickest method but should a perch float up again, the former technique is employed.

By mid-afternoon our mind-blowing perch bonanza was over as quickly as it had started and we couldn't buy another hit whatever the lure. It was time to move on and give the area a total rest. So the following morning we set a northerly route towards Aswan with a view to researching another of Tim's hunches. We were heading for an area similar in character to our previous venue, with boulders, rocky ridges and sunken islands, some 50 miles to the north. And when we finally arrived over the area in the late afternoon, dense beds of the same long, pointed, curly-leaved weed just happened to be covering the bottom. What a coincidence! For once I was pleased to retrieve a weed-covered lure when I recognized the plant responsible. It certainly looked promising and indicated that my theory of the big females gathering beside their eventual spawning sites as an early grouping process could just be right.

In less than an hour's trolling before darkness set in we accounted for several nice fish (all females), the largest of 75lb to Tim's rod, and pulled free from at least two more whoppers. During one hilarious ten-minute spell Tim and I actually found ourselves playing fish at the same time, when up popped a perch to grab my lure as I was retrieving to allow Tim room to play his perch – and we landed both too. What would our last morning on Lake Nasser bring? Would there be a mass of buffaloes here, attracted to the same pre-spawning habitat? After dinner all kinds of thoughts filled our conversation before we got our heads down early in preparation for a dawn start.

We agreed that midday was the latest that we could realistically continue to fish before making the long trip back to the moorings in Aswan and so we made the very most of our last session. After a slow start Tim finally got amongst the buffaloes, with our first fish of the day weighing 126lb – and what a superb scrap it put up. We even took time in setting up the trophy shots beside a small island where we could get in the water and help Tim display the perch – always the best option if shallow water is close by. Andy then took one of 103lb, while I had fish of 100lb, 60lb, 50lb and, would you believe, a 10-pounder, our smallest on the troll all week. Then I went and hit into what was obviously a really big vundu catfish which zoomed off over 100 yards of line, dived straight down and became impossible to budge from the rocky bottom where it had lodged itself, some 30 feet down. So after much cursing and applying leverage from every direction possible I had reluctantly to call it a day.

That's the wonder of Lake Nasser. I always pack my gear away wanting to return at the earliest possible opportunity. Our week's tally amounted to no fewer than ten Nile perch between 100 and 162lb being landed. And from a freshwater lake – that just has to be some kind of record. Moreover all were returned to do battle another day. It is interesting to note that despite their tiny, seemingly weak eyes, vundu catfish have no trouble whatsoever chasing and hitting even lures being trolled quite fast (probably due

Above *Following shore lunch provided by Rabbi, the chef on board the supply boat, enjoyed on a remote sandy-topped island (once the Nubian desert), Tim Baily and his boat guides discuss the afternoon's potential trolling and shore-fishing marks for my party of eight Nile perch enthusiasts from the UK. Sleeping on board under the stars, eating wholesome spicy local food and enjoying the chance of being a boy again for seven precious days, not to mention memorable battles with big perch or vundu catfish, is what attracts anglers to the silent remoteness of this truly enigmatic environment called Lake Nasser.*

to water clarity). In my opinion, most of the 'lost leviathan' stories of big Nile perch taking the unfortunate angler down into the rocks and breaking the line can be attributed to vundu in the 50-100lb size range. It is indeed an incredibly powerful adversary.

Concerning our trolling tackle both Andy and I were using my Masterline 9½-foot Voyager/uptide rods, he with one of the new ABU Morrum 7700 multiplying reels loaded with 30lb mono and myself a 10000 loaded with 35lb mono. That is standard tackle for trolling on the lake. Tim used a shorter, one-piece Muskie jerk bait rod, Calcutta 400 multiplier and 50lb fused braid. There is no doubt that being considerably thinner than say 35lb mono, braid of 40–50lb test permits lures to dive significantly deeper. In general terms I would say most lures work at least 2–3 feet deeper (sometimes even more) on braid than the equivalent breaking strain in monofilament. When working a lure at great lengths behind the boat and tacking an irregular course with the boat in order to fool spooky perch well away from its course, then braid is in a class of its own. There is far too much stretch in mono for the hooks to be driven home successfully at great distances. But overall I would still prefer the fight of a big fish to be on mono, even though one of my buffaloes did come to braid. I like the forgiving properties of monofilament and the fact that any nasty nicks or abrasive damage due to the line hitting rocks are instantly noticed during the fight and when retrieving the lure. With braid they are not always apparent, which no doubt results in those sudden inexplicable 'break-offs'. Then again with braid it's so easy to determine when even the slightest frond of weed is caught on the lure, such is the exaggerated, throbbing action of the rod tip transmitted from the artificial when trolling using a totally non-stretch line.

For the record, our catch (most of which were caught trolling in just three days) resulted in over 2,500lb of perch averaging in excess of 75lb apiece, with Andy and I boating over 1,000lb each. It was truly unbelievable fishing and could only happen on Lake Nasser.

THE BEAUTIFUL BAHAMAS

C hristopher Columbus landed in the Bahamas on 12 October 1492. The Islands of the Bahamas consists of a magical coral archipelago, bisected by the Tropic of Cancer. It stretches for over 650 miles from the east coast of Florida to the south-eastern tip of Cuba. It covers 100,000 square miles of shallow ocean plateaux and comprises 700 islands (only 30 of which are inhabited) and over 2,500 cays (tiny mangrove islands – pronounced 'keys') with a total land mass of just 5,300 square miles and a population of only 250,000, most of whom reside in the two main cities – Nassau on New Providence Island and Freeport on Grand Bahama.

It is small wonder that the Bahamas boast the most extensive and remote bonefish habitat in the world. Most of the islands are flat and carpeted in thick pine forests, mangrove swamps, lagoons and lakes and are completely surrounded by sparkling, powdery, white and pink sandy beaches where sandpipers, turkey vultures and ospreys, amongst many other bird species, are regular sightings. The Bahamas are everyone's idea of a 'Robinson Crusoe' existence and they provide an exotic, year-round, saltwater fly-fisherman's paradise.

Blue-water sport with, among others, dorado, wahoo, tunas and billfish, sailing, windsurfing, snorkelling and scuba diving can also be enjoyed should you tire of hooking into bonefish, arguably the world's fastest, most exhilarating, shallow-water saltwater sportsfish, which is justly labelled 'shadow of the flats'. Bonefish are decidedly barbel-shaped with firm silvery bodies that seem to absorb all the colours around them, giving them their unique and exceptional camouflage. When hooked, bonefish can rip off, in long unstoppable surges, over 100 yards of backing to follow your fly line across the flats, as you watch helplessly in total disbelief – the rod being held high above the head to prevent the leader from chaffing on rocks or coral. And these are just average-sized bones in the 3-6lb class. If you become attached to anything upwards of 9-10lb, you'll either be chasing after it like someone possessed or literally running fast out of backing. To hit the jackpot you are really looking for double-figure fish, which are not uncommon. Monsters in the 14-16lb range are, however, rare but present in sufficient numbers to attract the specialist fly rodder. This gives reason enough for not seeking bonefish without at least 200 yards of backing on your reel. Mine, a Youngs Sea Venture, is fitted with a saltwater disc drag and holds 250 yards of 30lb low-diameter Power Pro braid, plus a 35 yard WF9 floating Cortland 444 Tropic Plus lazer line. This unique line has a special hard coating so that it stays stiff in the heat of the tropics, which is a point worth considering because most standard floating lines go all soft and sloppy when exposed to extreme heat and become difficult to cast. Frankly, whilst you can effectively fly fish for bonefish using a standard British powerful reservoir rod and reel outfit, simply 'palming' fish on the run if the reel lacks an effective drag system (I caught hundreds of fish in this way during my early bonefishing days), trying to cast with a soft or sticky line is a nightmare.

The rod I use nowadays is my own John Wilson 10-foot Heritage saltwater fly rod. This three-piece model stashes away easily in the overhead compartment in the plane. In addition to bonefish, the same rod has accounted for pike and carp to over 20lb plus bass, mullet and even salmon to 25lb in British Columbia. Incidentally, to the end of the fly line I sleeve on a 'big butt' leader (using the braided tube and silicon sleeve provided) to which I add a tippet of 8-10lb fluorocarbon. I find the rapidly tapering mono aids turnover enormously, especially when casting into the wind, though contrary to popular belief distance casting is not the secret to hooking spooky bonefish. What is of paramount importance however, and in this order, is observation, stealth and opportunism, followed by short to medium extremely accurate casts, casting sideways low to the water when necessary to avoid fish-frightening 'flashes' of the rod from overhead movements.

Previous spread *Being whisked along at forty knots in a powerful speedboat across warm aquamarine shallows, where exotic birds are regular sightings, is holiday enough for some. To fly rodders visiting the beautiful Bahamas, however, it is merely the start of each and every day's exhilarating sight casting for what is arguably the planet's fastest inshore saltwater sportsfish – the incredible bonefish.*

Above *Even modest-sized bonefish can rip over 100 yards of backing from your reel. As most are hooked in*

less than twenty-four inches of water, they cannot dive so they run and run and run like a bat out of hell. No species, save for the permit, also found on these shallow crystal-clear flats, can possibly hold a candle to the bonefish in terms of speed, power and camouflage. Their wiry, silvery bodies seem to absorb all the colours around them, making bonefish by far the hardest fish to identify against the sea floor even through polaroid glasses, particularly at distance.

To moving bonefish the fly should be landed several feet ahead and slightly beyond the fish so that when retrieved it crosses its path well within vision. To bonefish 'tailing' in really shallow water any fly (and lightweight patterns are most desirable here) gently dropped a foot or two to the side of the fish's head is liable to be pounced upon instantly. Sure, you can catch bonefish casting blind into an area of what the guides call 'grey water' which denotes a large shoal of usually modest-sized fish disturbing the mud in search of their favourite food, the blue crab – their distinctive 'pug' or 'nose' marks clearly visible on the bottom once the silt settles. But who wants to cast blind when you can visually stalk individual specimen-sized bonefish or small pods of just several large fish utilizing your skill and watercraft in sight-casting to pick out the biggest? Should the sun suddenly go in or a heavy ripple get up for a while, most experienced guides simply stop fishing, shove their pole into the bottom and wait – clarity of water and maximum vision for the angler is that important. Depending upon bottom structure, whether it is light or dark sand or mud covered in grass, or a broken mixture of rocks, sand and grass, the bonefish is never the easiest of fishes to define, even in full sunshine.

In overcast conditions, it could almost be swimming beneath the boat before your eyes have located it. An effective pair of Polaroid glasses and a peaked hat are therefore imperative. I also wear a pair of lightweight, easy-to-flick-off shoes, so that should a fish go charging through the mangroves I can hop overboard instantly in pursuit.

Undoubtedly once you are competent, you will delight in walking the shallow flats alone or with a friend searching for bonefish. It gives you the most wonderful carefree feeling in the world, and a tip here is to lift each foot completely clear of the water whilst

Above *Watched by my boat partner, Henry Waszczuk of Canadian Sportsfishing Productions, during a media day out following the World Invitational Bonefishing Championships held on the Island of Exuma back in October 1997, in*

which I was fortunate to take third place, I am finally starting to recover line from a big bonefish following several powerful surges which evaporated over 150 yards of backing from the reel. Yes the inshore flats are really this colour and as clear as gin.

wading to within casting distance of fish, pointing your toes downwards in order to create the absolute minimum of disturbance. Haphazard wading and sloshing about will frighten off a pod of bones from over 100 yards away. It's worth remembering that most of the bonefish you catch will be hooked in less than 24 inches of water.

Initially, though, no one can learn without the help and experience of a professional guide who will zip you across turquoise reefs and over pearl-white shallow flats in his 16- to 18-foot flat-bottomed skiff at speeds approaching 40 miles an hour from one

hot spot to another. These customized craft come fitted with a flat unobstructed foredeck (for casting), integral tackle storage and optional high poling platforms. So from an elevated position providing maximum vision of the flats ahead, the guide can pole you silently along to within casting distance of even the spookiest bonefish. Most models accommodate engines in the 50-115hp range and are fitted with hydraulic twin tabs, although hulls on certain models are designed to keep the bulk of the weight on centreline, and as far forward as possible, thus eliminating the need for twin tabs.

Sometimes you'll simply drift with the wind while the guide steadies the skiff for casting with the long pole. At other times he'll have to work hard pushing you across the flats to intercept a pod of bonefish he saw from over 100 yards off. Yes! The Bahamian guides are that good. And only when you have managed to spot a fish or group of fish before he does will you begin to understand a guide's real worth. On most days you'll also see huge stingrays by the dozen and numerous sharks at close quarters – lemon and black tips especially – the occasional tarpon or permit, maybe a group of jacks, and most certainly barracuda. I once saw a sawfish fully ten feet long. Losing a hooked bonefish to sharks and especially barracuda is not uncommon.

Of course, like I do, there is nothing to stop you from taking along a heavy spinning rod and multiplier combo loaded with 20lb mono. The guide will assume you are

Above *The iridescent silver sheen of the bonefish when viewed out of the water is rather misleading. Below the surface its scales take on colours of the immediate surroundings in a similar way to those of the permit and barracuda. Note the distinct eye, large barbel-like pectoral fins and cavernous underslung mouth. It is customary to use barbless-hook flies and to immediately release all bonefish once they have recovered their strength.*

bonkers, on account of Bahamian waters being blessed with such an array of exotic super sportsfish. Nevertheless a big silver spoon, floating Rapala Magnum or imitation needlefish lure connected to a wire trace, will provide great sport with sizeable barracudas. Alternatively you can add a large streamer fly or a needle fish barracuda fly and wire trace to your leader. Barracudas really explode from the surface and have amazing speed. No doubt your guide will then also start to become interested!

A large percentage of bonefish flies (all the guides carry a bag of varying patterns for sale) are based upon the famous Crazy Charlie, a pattern tied with a pair of bead, brass or even lead eyes (for deep water) on top of the shank of a size 8-2 hook (so it fishes upside-down and doesn't catch bottom or weed) to resemble the shrimp upon which bonefish feed. My favourite pattern is the Gotcha Special, tied with a glitter pearl tail and body, long pink throat hairs and chain eyes. It represents perfectly that pinkish hue of the natural shrimp.

Now comes the strangest part of fly fishing for bonefish, which is in complete contrast to catching trout: the retrieve. You point the rod tip low down directly at the fish and strip a couple of short sharp jerks to get its attention. If it follows, you allow time for it to suck in the artificial between each couple of strips, before stripping again (6- to 12-inch pulls) and only when you can feel the resistance of its weight on the end, do you pull the hook point home, then raise the rod into a full bend as the bonefish belts off at devastating speed. Should it miss the fly after a few strips, pause and keep stripping with pauses in between. Don't on any account lift the rod high or to the side as if British

Below *My bonefishing outfit. A ten-foot three-piece Masterline Heritage saltwater fly rod, Youngs Sea Venture disc drag saltwater reel, holding a WF9 floating Cortland 444 Tropic Plus Lazer Line, plus 250 yards of 30lb low-diameter Power Pro braided backing. My fly box contains a mixture of patterns many based upon the chain-eyed Crazy Charlie shrimp imitation with throat hairs of pink and glitter pearl body. Note also the needlefish imitation barracuda flies, over five inches long.*

Previous spread *These turquoise-blue waters stretching out from the poolside complex at the Radisson Cable Beach Hotel on the island of Nassau typify what visiting fly-fishermen can expect. Along with generous Bahamian hospitality and luxury facilities there is a wonderful sense of 'getting away from it all'. Tell your guide you want to totally chill out and you won't see or hear another living soul all day through.*

Left *My good friend and fellow angling journalist Walt Jennings, from Venice in Florida, displays the frightening canine teeth of a modest-sized barracuda. Such fish provide great alternative flats sport to bonefish whether using fly or spinning tackle. Their speed, agility and acrobatic skills are legendary. Note their similar colours to that of the bonefish on page 27.*

trout fishing. You'll simply pull the fly away and the bonefish will lose interest. As long as the rod is kept low while you continue to strip, the bonefish will keep following until it either inhales the fly or sees the boat, panics and shoots off. Bonefish do not rush at a fly and zoom off all in one go like a rainbow trout, and thus snap the line being stripped through a straight rod; rather they stop to 'munch' which is when you pull to set the hook. Then all hell breaks loose.

Having been spoilt for choice over the past few years whilst sampling numerous lodges in the Bahamas, I would like to recommend the following islands and lodges. On the largest island of Andros, which incidentally has the third largest barrier reef in the world, I have enjoyed superb sportsfishing out from Small Hope Bay Lodge, Kamalame Cove, Andros Island Bone Fishing Club, Charlie's Haven at Behring Point and Bair Bahamas guesthouse. In the Exhumas, the famous Club Peace and Plenty at Georgetown managed by Bob Hyde has experienced guides to show you all around this 90-mile-long chain of islands where the James Bond movies *Thunderball* and *Never Say Never Again* were both filmed. In Abaco, both Netties Different of Abaco and The Bonefish Paradise at Sandy Point offer wonderful sport in totally unspoilt surroundings. On Grand Bahama, I recommend both the Deep Water Cay fishing lodge, managed by Paul and Alison Adams, and North Riding Point ,run by Ben and Judy Rose. But frankly wherever you book up to fly fish in the Bahamas you will be well catered for and undoubtedly catch bonefish. Overall the best months are April or May, with October and November a close second, though really any time of the year will guarantee an exciting holiday.

Lastly, most of the islands airports can be reached direct from Miami, following a long-haul nine-hour flight from Heathrow or Gatwick. The only direct flight from the UK lands in Nassau, the Bahamian centre of commerce and tourism which boasts some wonderful hotels including the outlandish Atlantis, a veritable marine extravaganza in terms of its massive walk-around saltwater aquariums (the largest in the world) which display most of the species you are likely to encounter. Did I forget to mention the casinos and night clubs, and that favourite local dishes include the succulent white flesh of the conch shell, plus stuffed peppered crabs and sumptuous crawfish? There's a great local beer too, and what about those colourful and exotic intoxicating cocktails. As they say in the Bahamas, 'it just keeps getting better'!

JOHN WILSON'S GREATEST FISHING ADVENTURES

THE GAMBIA
WEST AFRICA

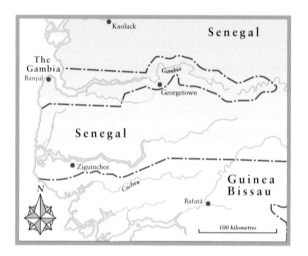

Rich and yet poor in so many ways; harsh yet beautiful. The hallmark and stark images of Africa, together with its many different peoples, cultures, languages, exotic perfumes and diversity of flora and fauna make this continent utterly fascinating. And you'll find it all here in one of her tiniest, most colourful children, The Gambia. Geographically this vibrant country is narrowly wedged into West Africa's Senegal, with tourism fast becoming its major industry due to the English-speaking people, wonderful year-round climate and golden sandy beaches dotted with affordable hotels and colourful fishing villages.

The real heart of the country is the fabulously rich and coloured, shrimp-packed Gambia River, which flows westwards for over 400 miles from its source in Guinea Bissau, finally emptying into the Atlantic Ocean at Banjul, the capital. Here in the five-mile-wide mouth of the river, where depths vary from just 10 to over 60 feet, schools of bottle-nosed dolphins delight tourists and anglers alike, and the strong tidal influences prevail for some 200 miles upriver all the way to Georgetown. Stretching inland from the delta around Banjul is a huge, fascinating network of mangrove swamps and tidal channels attracting many fish species including tarpon, ninebones, crevalle jacks, barracudas and captain fish, plus a host of colourful and quaint lesser species from butter fish and red snappers to the tooth-laden bastard halibut. And the exotic bird life provides a veritable twitcher's paradise, with ospreys, goliath herons and bee-eaters considered everyday sightings.

Boat fishing charters, whether fun trips through the maze of creeks in a traditional gaily painted pirogue (great sport using shrimps on light carp or spinning-style tackle) or off-shore reef fishing at anchor, trolling, shark fishing, among others, all start at Denton Bridge a few miles south of the capital. Here the main coastal road from Banjul spans a wide and fast tidal channel where all the boats are anchored, providing skippers with a quick route out into the ocean, or a chug through mangrove channels (trolling for barracuda *en route*) into Banjul harbour and all upriver destinations. Prior to setting off, a tub of fresh livebaits in the way of 4-6-inch yaboos, a silver-sided herring-like fish, are easily taken adjacent to Denton Bridge by anchoring a little uptide and jigging with a set of hook-eye shrimp lures. Alternatively, live mullet may be purchased from the cast net fishermen who work the shallows beside the bridge every morning. Also from the local fish markets, fresh bonga fish (an allis shad no less and the staple food fish of The Gambia) are always cheaply available for whole or cut bait.

On the social side, you can order sumptuous seafood cocktails in the way of jumbo-sized curried shrimps and grilled lobsters, whilst lazing beside your hotel pool. So it's not difficult to understand why, being less than six hours away from Gatwick, anglers are now flocking to The Gambia, and they are returning year after year. My wife, Jo, and I have it at the very top of our holiday list. For unequalled lunchtime pleasure there is nothing to beat Il Mondos at Kotu beach just seven miles south of Banjul where, along with lobsters and giant shrimps, visitors can enjoy a pitcher of delicious sangria or a Special Pitcher made from calvados, amaretto, cointreau, dry cider and crushed ice. Small wonder I can never fathom out which mix I like best.

As for the fishing, I need to go back to the late 1980s when I first met Yorkshireman Mark Longster, now by far the most experienced and respected of all Gambian charter skippers. In those early days when filming for television, Mark made an enormous effort to ensure that we caught large sharks whilst anchored in the middle of the river mouth at Baraa. We accounted for lemon sharks to over 300lb, plus some large barracudas on two consecutive days. Strangely, shark fishing is now largely forgotten in Gambian waters; it has been replaced with a growing interest in giant tarpon and unbelievably exciting reef fishing for a dozen or more species that can top 30lb. And with his current boats *Tarpon 1* and *Tarpon 2*, which are beamy, 21-foot Wilson Flyers sporting 50hp

outboard engines, Mark and his partner, Tracey Day, through their company Gambian Fishing, now offer several exciting packages to the visiting fisherman.

I guess overall that reef fishing at anchor over the rocks either at Baraa or further south over the mantle reef, provide the best 'bran tub' sport of all. Whilst ledgering out bonga bait or a livebait on a 20-30lb class outfit, likely customers include the colourful and absurdly hard-fighting cubera snapper to over 30lb, crevalle jacks to over 25lb, cassarvas (known as kob in South Africa) up to 40lb and the strange (transparent-nosed) king threadfin salmon, also called captain fish, but known locally as kujeli. These fast-running super sportsfish are regularly caught in the 30-50lb bracket on small livebaits, yaboos or mullet (and the world's all-tackle best of 72lb was in fact successfully recorded in The Gambia). Incidentally, and this illustrates the potential of these incredible fertile seas, whilst shark fishing off Baraa in 50 feet of water during the early days before anyone in The Gambia bothered about IGFA records, Mark caught a truly mammoth threadfin salmon weighing 120lb, using a whole bonga fish as bait on a 10/0 hook and wire trace – but never bothered to claim the capture as a record.

The same can be said of another species, the cobia, also occasionally caught in the 40-70lb bracket by anglers fishing over the mantle reef. A huge cobia, weighing 154lb (20lb above the current IGFA record) was taken by English angler, Bob Murrock, whilst trolling a CD18 plug for barracudas at the back of the Sunwing Hotel. The capture was

Left *After being towed up and down the five-mile-wide Gambia River, off Baraa at Banjul, for three hours this world-record-shattering 303lb tarpon eventually succumbed to the rod of Bedfordshire angler Carl Pashley, left. No wonder both he and skipper Mark Longster have celebratory drinks in their hands. As so often happens, unfortunately, the American-based International Game Fishing Association decided in their infinite wisdom not to accept the eight-foot-long monster as an all-tackle world record, despite it being weighed ashore on reputable scales, and all knots and rigs being tied by Carl himself. He was even holding the rod when the giant tarpon engulfed his double yaboos (small shad) live baits. Neither angler would have dreamed of killing the specimen to be verified had they not been certain of it shattering the 283lb world-record tarpon caught in Venezuela in 1956.*

Next spread *A 40lb stingray is not the easiest salt-water species to hold. Norman Message from Eastbourne receives some experienced local help with his prize winning fish during the three-day second Masterline International West African Shore Championships held in The Gambia during November 2000, along the famous Sanyang Surf beach eighteen miles south of Banjul.*

in fact recorded on video, but not ratified by the IGFA due to a mix-up during the exhaustive ratification form-filling process. There are, however, several Gambian records accepted by the IGFA including the all-tackle sandbar shark of 260lb caught by Paul Delsignore in 1989. But none can compare with a truly giant barracuda (commercially taken unfortunately) which Mark witnessed at Bakau fish market, having been already hacked into three easy-to-weigh pieces. Together the head and two body chunks totalled a staggering 60kg, which despite losing an enormous amount of body fluids, came from a colossal barracuda easily 40lb heavier than the current world all-tackle record of 83lb caught by K. Hackett from Lagos, Nigeria in 1952. Some of the best trolling for both barracudas and crevalle jacks, incidentally, is also along the reefs running parallel with the southern coastline, and in Mark's opinion the most successful artificial lure of all is the Rapala CD18 in either blue mackerel or redhead – a preference I would say that skippers share on a world-wide basis in both fresh and saltwater.

Now let's talk about tarpon fishing 'Gambia style'. Again monsters far larger than the long-standing current all-tackle world IGFA record of 283lb (caught from Lake Maracaibo in Venezuela in 1956 by M. Salazar) not only exist but in large numbers in the Gambia River. The largest authenticated tarpon weighed an incredible 303lb and was landed following a three-hour battle by Carl Pashley from England using a 55lb test braided reel line (it was refused by the IGFA on a technicality, despite being officially weighed).

With reference to there being real numbers of huge tarpon living in the Gambia River however, I recall a session of several years back when Jo and I visited Mark and Tracey for a week's serious fishing. We had motored upriver to opposite Dog Island and anchored in the middle of a 50-foot deep tide rip where the Gambia River is getting on for 12 miles across. (This is a known tarpon channel where anything can in fact turn up, like the 115lb cubera snapper in 1997 which gobbled up a single yaboo intended for tarpon, the angler needing all of his 50lb line class outfit to subdue such a massive cubera.) During the last two hours of the flood tide Mark was convinced we would experience tarpon breaking the mirror-like surface and together with a group of bottle-nosed dolphins, he was so right. Massive tarpon could be seen wallowing and crashing through the surface film for at least a couple of hundred yards in all four directions around the boat. Scarcely a minute passed by without one, two or even three monsters simultaneously rolling, topping and tailing or crashing out. There were obviously hundreds, if not a thousand plus, monstrous tarpon all around us – huge deep-bodied specimens, between 7 and 8 feet long in the 150-300lb range. I have never experienced such a spectacle of massive fish ever before or since. We were like kids in a sweet shop and expected any second for one of our four freelined mullet livebaits to go screeching off. Suddenly Mark hooked up with a fish of well over 200lb but after a 20-minute battle it got away.

Around two years later, Mark and I were anchored in more or less the same position off Dog Island, this time sharing the boat with Don Metcalfe, who hooked up with no fewer than three huge tarpon within a mad hour's spell one after another, pulling out of each following that initial jump or two.

Personally I have actually still yet to land one of The Gambia's huge tarpon, but it doesn't stop me from trying. Incidentally, and coming down in size to much smaller tarpon within the 25-70lb range, there is some fabulous action to be had during the Gambian summer months, June through to September, throughout the rainy season. It's humid and wet, but nice. The rain is not of the monsoon type, merely short, heavy bursts. And during this period tarpon in plenty can be hooked using jigs, lures, and livebaits, even on fly from around the rocks off Cape Point, just south of Banjul.

For a totally different Gambian experience, from December through until April, Mark arranges five- or seven-day trips by Land Rover to the high upper reaches of the Gambia River, way above Georgetown at McCarthy Island known locally as 'Janh Janh Bara'. Here the river is between 200 and 300 yards across, scattered with islands, sandbars and reefs and overhung along the margins by tall hardwood trees. The are baboons, monkeys, plus an unbelievable diversity of bird life along with crocodiles and hippos. This is the original slave-trading island settlement of the colonial days where, in addition to many of the previously mentioned saltwater species, tooth-laden tiger fish, several catfish species, and elephant snout fish plus dozens of weird and wonderfully colourful species can be taken using fresh shrimp or fish strip.

In complete contrast to these upriver safaris, and for groups of up to six anglers, how about a day trip over to Bijlo Island? This is a flat, low-lying island comprising rocky outcrops and sandbars where myriad birds reside including pelicans, storks, egrets, herons, terns and plovers, just half a mile offshore from Tangi Fishing Village on the south coast, 15 miles from Banjul. A 15-minute boat trip by traditional pirogue puts you on to this fascinating bird sanctuary (the noise is deafening as you arrive) where jacks, barracudas, and snappers are readily caught amongst the rocks on artificial lures, particularly shallow-running plugs such as the Rapala J13, and on toby lures which have had the treble hook replaced by a large single. The jacks especially love surface poppers. For bottom-bait enthusiasts using standard beach gear, guitar fish and stingrays feature regularly on the incoming tide. In fact anyone considering shore-fishing in The Gambia would do well to remember that usually the most prolific sport is during that last three hours of the flooding tide. From the surf beaches south of Banjul, Mark had in years past taken both guitar fish and stingrays exceeding 100lb using fresh small whole squid or small fish for bait, on more or less standard British shore-fishing gear and a 25lb reel line. So we were both intrigued as to what would be caught during the three days of the Masterline International sponsored West African Shore Championships held in The Gambia during November 2000, along the golden sands and bass-like surf waves of Sanyang Beach, some 18 miles south of the capitol Banjul.

With £5,000 of tackle vouchers to be won plus big money optional pools, the 70 competitors from all over Britain and Ireland were split up into three sections which were rotated over the three days. Having already agreed with competition

Right *Finally plucked from the foaming surf at Sanyang Beach, this chunky 20lb guitar fish, otherwise known as shovel-nosed ray, put up a tremendous scrap for Ray Brant, a shore-fisherman from Basildon, Essex, during the Masterline International West African Shore Championship. Many a larger specimen was lost, however. This particular species, which gives birth to live young, attains weights and lengths well in excess of 100lb and seven feet.*

Below *The Gambia is indeed a twitcher's paradise, with ospreys, goliath herons, bee-eaters, and a myriad of wading birds everyday sightings. Even vultures can be viewed at close quarters.*

Left *The big barracuda is one of the meanest and most impressive predators inhabiting the rich waters of The Gambia. My good friend Don Metcalfe hooked into this magnificent forty-five pounder which measured over five feet long, using mullet livebait, from the wide mouth of the river at Baraa, just off Banjul. Believe it or not monsters weighing almost three times this size have been caught by local commercial fishermen.*

Right *The broad smiles of its children are evident wherever you travel in The Gambia.*

organizers, John Prescott of Countryman Angling, and Richard Sheard of World Sports Fishing, to both open and close the event with a prize-giving evening, Masterline's marketing director, Chris Leibbrandt and I felt decidedly frustrated merely walking the three sections without a rod in our hands each day instead of competing. Sometimes there were so many fish being caught I couldn't decide which direction to point my camera lens next. I felt particularly sorry for Colin Palliser from Dublin who, after playing a huge guitar fish looking all of 70lb plus for over half an hour, had his line parted when the spent fish was almost on the beach by an enthusiastic local helper, who I nicknamed the 'gaffman from hell'. Another titanic battle which literally went right down to the wire was mail-order tackle guru, Tony Kirrage's encounter with what was obviously a huge stingray looking well in excess of 100lb. Again, the result was a botched gaffing attempt. So Tony watched his good friend Norman Message from Eastbourne receive the biggest fish of the festival prize for a 40lb stingray knowing he had almost landed its granddad. Frankly I could not stop wondering what might have been beached had some of the competitors gone for broke with a size 5/0 hook offering a large bonga fillet or small whole squid as bait, on a 25lb-test reel line, instead of two and three small fine-wire hook traces to just a 15lb-test reel line – the mind boggles. But then paradoxically top man over the three-day event was John O'Brien from Waterford in Ireland who not only caught far more fish than anyone else, at the competition rules of 5 points per fish and 10 points per kilo, his 17lb kujeli was the biggest landed. During the couple of days prior to and immediately after the beach tournament, many of the competitors also experienced some memorable boat fishing trips in the Gambia River. Nigel Lloyd and his 12-year-old son took it in turns to successfully land a massive tarpon hooked near Dog Island which was returned and estimated after measuring at around 220lb. What unbelievable sport The Gambia has to offer.

THE FRASER RIVER

BRITISH COLUMBIA, CANADA

The famous Fraser River system is one of the largest in North America, next to the Mississippi. Situated in south-central British Columbia in the south-west of Canada, it flows north-west, south and west through spectacular canyons in the Coast Mountains to the Strait of Georgia. It remains undammed throughout its 850-mile course and thus ranks as one of the world's last great salmon-producing rivers. It is a truly historical wonderland where aboriginal people fished for salmon 12,000 years ago and where, in centuries past, the run of sockeye salmon alone amounted to 100 million fish annually. Although those days are long gone, the Fraser River still has no equal in its migratory salmon runs.

Back in the 1950s when, like many a teenager of my generation, I became musically influenced by the likes of skiffle and blue grass, one of my all-time favourite inspirational songs was the *Grand Coulee Dam*, immortalized by Lonnie Donnegan. I still remember most of the words telling the story of the mighty Columbia River and how the Grand Coulee Dam was created to provide hydroelectricity for the production of chrome, manganese and white aluminium. Little was I to know then, however, that 40 years later in the early 1990s, whilst *en route* from Winnipeg to Vancouver during the filming of my international *Go Fishing* programmes for Anglia Television, I would be looking down from the flight deck of an airliner through the white puffy clouds at the famous Canadian Rocky Mountains and the headwaters of the Columbia River. Words from the song 'she comes roaring down the canyons' – 'tore their boats to splinters' – 'and gave man dreams to dream' – 'but river while you're rambling, you can do some work for me' immediately came flooding back from those formative teenage years. Strangely the Canadian pilot couldn't remember the song.

From Vancouver the *Go Fishing* crew then flew north to the logging town of Terrace where, from the glacial-fed Skeena and Copper rivers, I caught on fly dolly varden

Previous spread *What kind of freshwater fish does it take six strong Canadians to attempt lifting for the camera? An eleven-foot two-inch white sturgeon, that's what. This awesome specimen had the immense girth of sixty-six inches and was estimated to weigh in excess of 900lb. It was caught from the Fraser River near Chilliwack in British Columbia in 1998 by Harry Watson (second on left) whose guide that day, Fred Helmer of Fred's Fishing Adventures, specializes in organized sturgeon- and salmon-fishing trips on both the Fraser and Harrison Rivers, using*

super-fast twenty-foot aluminium jet boats and a team of experienced local guides.

Above *Amongst breathtaking scenery at the point where the Harrison River converges with the mighty Fraser, retired police officer Andy Hardy from London bends into his umpteenth salmon of the morning. These included chum, chinook and cohos, all on a lightweight spinning outfit, using back-bouncing, trotting and spinning techniques. Small wonder the Fraser River boasts the largest runs of migratory salmon in the world.*

(a char), pink salmon and steelhead trout. It was a marvellous experience and left me thinking that if I was a young man again I would be thinking very seriously indeed about emigrating to the wilderness countryside and pristine, untamed landscapes of Canada's Pacific north-west.

That feeling had not changed one iota when ten years later in October 2000 I revisited Vancouver in the company of Christine Slater and Andy Hardy to fish for the legendary white sturgeon (*Acipenzer transmontanus*) of the Fraser River system. There are also five separate species of Pacific salmon running up the Fraser. The coho, which averages 3-8lb, the pink which runs in huge concentrations every other year and averages 5-7lb, the colourful sockeye, most common in the 5-12lb bracket, the powerful chum, also called dog salmon, which is 15-20lb, and the largest by far of them all, the chinook with recorded weights exceeding 100lb. Locally it is also referred to as white and spring salmon and can range anywhere from 10 to over 50lb. Oh, and if that's not enough to go at, there are steelhead trout (sea-running rainbows) in the 5-25lb category. As bizarre as it may seem however to the visiting sturgeon angler, these are simply bonus species to be enjoyed on light tackle when you have had your fill of arm-wrenching

battles with arguably the planet's largest freshwater fish. I say arguably because some of
the white sturgeon inhabiting the Fraser system are known to be anadromous, in that
they spend a proportion of their life in the Pacific Ocean and part in freshwater, whereas
most never actually leave and spend their entire existence in freshwater. How big do
they grow? The largest commercially caught white sturgeon (there is a much smaller
rarely caught species – the green sturgeon) from the Fraser system was way back in
the 1940s and weighed a staggering 1387lb. In more recent years in 1976, a 12½-foot
monster, caught by Fred Helman and his brother, topped the 1,000lb mark, though they
had to cut the giant fish into several chunks in order to weigh it. Nowadays of course
there is no commercial fishing for sturgeon and all are protected by a catch-and-release
policy allowing them to fight another day. (It is interesting to note that from the mighty
Columbia River in Oregon back in the 1950s a mammoth white sturgeon weighing in
excess of 1,800lb was taken commercially. Teams of mules were once used to haul these
great fish from the river, and some teams were reportedly lost during such mammoth
tugs of war.)

Christine, Andy and I made our base at Chilliwack, 70 miles east of Vancouver,
where Fred Helmer runs a custom tackle shop and guiding service specializing in
freshwater expeditions for both salmon and sturgeon throughout the Fraser Valley. It

Above *I needed serious help from good friend Andy Hardy (left), and experienced guide Greg Heaps (middle), to hoist my largest white sturgeon of the week for a trophy shot. They are such incredibly long fish to display. This beauty was estimated at around 170 – 180lb and succumbed to a ledgered ball of fresh salmon eggs wrapped in a piece of fine-mesh ladies' tights. Honestly! This is the bait par excellence although lamprey heads or small whitefish are also taken.*

is very well organized. One of Fred's guides (and we fished with four different, all exceedingly knowledgeable guys, during our week's stay) picks you up from your hotel in a 4 x 4, towing a 21-foot long, 6½-foot beam aluminium jet boat (equipped with all the tackle you are likely to need) and sporting an inboard 5-litre engine (some have 130hp outboards). Then, following a ten-minute drive, he's launching the boat from Island 22 on the outskirts of Chilliwack. Here the Fraser River is simply breathtaking, between 200 and 500 yards wide, extremely fast flowing and anywhere between just 5 and 80 feet deep. Its grandeur and beauty, being bordered throughout by steep, tree-covered and snow-topped mountains, has to be seen to be believed. And it's full of sturgeon and salmon, plus a variety of lesser species such as cutthroat and rainbow trout, dolly varden, whitefish and sculpin (a large bullhead).

Joining the Fraser just a few miles upstream is the clear-flowing Harrison River, also full of salmon and sturgeon, and much used by Fred's guides and local anglers alike. It runs for a distance of 8 miles to merge with the Fraser from its source which is massive Harrison Lake, itself 42 miles in length. There is just so much potential to go at, the mind boggles.

The guides whisk you along at between 30 and 40 knots to a variety of mind-blowing locations in both the Harrison and Fraser rivers, and the beauty of boat fishing is that

if nothing's doing at a particular spot, you're up and away and fishing again some place else within minutes, often covering as many as a dozen completely different locations in a day. Everywhere the mountainsides are stacked with a mixture of evergreens and deciduous trees, including giant firs, hemlock, cedar and pine, cottonwood, poplars, silver birch and maple. Land-based creatures and likely sightings include black bear, black-tailed deer, cougar, racoons and mink. The paw prints of coyotes can be seen on most sandbars where gulls, cranes and bald eagles make use of the continual salmon harvest for, with the exception of steelhead trout which run again to sea after spawning, all five salmon die after propagating their own kind. At varying times of the year, particularly in the autumn when the trees are a colourful patchwork of greens, yellows and burnt orange as the leaves of deciduous species fall to the ground, the riverbanks are a veritable graveyard of rotting carcasses. Yet these dead salmon, stinking by the thousand, help to form a valuable nutrient chain used by both hatching salmon fry and riverside vegetation alike. It is nothing other than nature's way of replenishing her food stocks, although the sight of countless salmon in their death throes may appear distasteful to city dwellers.

On our first day's fishing our guide, Greg Hunt, motored up the Harrison River to get us broken in on sturgeon and anchored up in a mid-river channel some 50 feet deep, immediately downstream from Harrison Lake. It was a truly breathtaking spot in a narrow gorge, stacked steeply along both banks by dense fir forest, the lower branches

Left *This wide bend on the picturesque Harrison River is typical of the local landscape, where down-current ledgering at anchor for white sturgeon averaging 100lb-plus is a most leisurely affair. That's until one of the rods starts knocking gently. Then all hell breaks loose as the fish is struck and comes completely clear of the surface at the end of its first powerful run.*

being favourite roosts to a pair of bald eagles, which were continually circling the boat for signs of a free meal. We put four rods out, each comprising a powerful one-piece 8½-foot all-through action Lamiglas 1024 blank, Shimano TLD20 multiplier reel loaded with 100lb-test braid and a 3-foot 80lb mono hook trace (some guides prefer Dacron or braid traces), the 7/0 Gamagatsu hook with its barb crunched down (barbless hooks are mandatory) presenting an eggball gently nicked on. Running above the trace swivel was a running slido (lead link) holding an 8oz weight. In short we were using a simple running rig. (An eggball is simply a bunch of fresh pinkish-red chum or chinook salmon eggs – each the size of a pea – neatly wrapped in a piece of fine-mesh ladies' tights, secured by several wraps of elasticated cotton, slightly smaller than the size of a golf ball. Apparently all the guides purchase their tights from the same store where the staff have for a long time stopped giving out old-fashioned looks.) With four long sensory barbels situated immediately ahead of its underslung, protrusile skate-like mouth, the white sturgeon is purpose built for hoovering up salmon eggs from the gravel bottom (hence their effectiveness) plus small fishes, crayfish and even the carcasses of dead salmon.

Within minutes we experienced the gentle tapping on the rod tips from interested sturgeon, interspersed with violent unmistakable vibrating knocks from whitefish and bullheads. With sturgeon the rod tip taps slowly away often for a minute or two before a positive bite develops. So it pays to lift the rod gently from the holder and point it towards the biting sturgeon until the line tightens fully. All hell then breaks loose when you strike and the hook is felt. Though Andy had caught these unique fish before and warned me of what might happen, I was barely ready for my first strike as a 100lb-plus sturgeon more than 6 feet in length, zoomed up from the bottom to perform a Polaris-style acrobatic leap not 30 yards from the boat (completely clearing the water in a thunderous shower of spray before diving down deep). Talk about getting your adrenaline going. There then followed an arm-wrenching scrap lasting all of 15 minutes which included a couple more spectacular leaps and several long, searing runs before I could begin to muscle this extremely powerful adversary up and alongside the boat. What a fish.

It was then I realized that white sturgeon are not in fact white. The long cartilaginous, prehistoric-looking almost shark-like body was streamlined, firm to the touch and a mixture of slate grey to brown along the back. Five rows of diamond-shaped armoured denticles, called scutes, run the fish's entire length: one line of spines down the dorsal crease ending at the dorsal fin itself, which is set far back near the tail; one line each side following the lateral line; one line along each side of the creamy white belly. The body itself is distinctly rough and sandpapery like that of a shark, as is the large upper tail lobe. It is a superbly proportioned creature and I was more than pleased on breaking the ton with my first sturgeon which measured 76 inches from the tip of its pointed snout to the fork of its tail. This put its weight at around 130lb. (All sturgeon are measured and their corresponding approximate weight taken from a length-to-weight chart in order to cause minimum stress to such a large fish rather than being hoisted on to scales in a sling. The chart puts a 50-inch sturgeon at 37lb, a 100-inch fish at 312lb and a 150-inch monster at 1,067lb.)

Once we had settled down again and put all four rods out with fresh bait balls it wasn't long before Christine became attached to her first sturgeon. I rather think the ensuing fight surprised her and this is a lady who has blue marlin of over 800lb under her belt. Being only slightly shorter than mine Christine's too logged in at over 100lb and also treated us to some acrobatic antics. There's simply no doubt about it, sturgeon of all sizes are great value for money. Most leap upon feeling cold steel and, as we were to discover throughout our week's safari, 100-200lb specimens are literally everyday catches on both the Harrison and Fraser rivers, with a very fair chance of hooking into something much, much larger – twice, three or even four times the size.

To end our first sturgeon session Andy took strike position (we took it in turns on the rods) and in came another 100lb-plus specimen. I was extremely impressed. Greg, our guide, then suggested we head back down the Harrison into the more coloured water of the Fraser for a spot of 'bottom bouncing' for salmon. Yet more spectacular fishing in this wonderful land was about to unfold as we weighed anchor and headed towards the wide expanse of the Fraser River.

As 'bottom bouncing' is a shore technique, Greg gunned the boat up on to a long bank of gravel where salmon could be seen on their way upriver in an extremely fast and shallow run just 30 yards out. He already had three 9-foot spinning rods rigged up with fixed spool reels and 15lb braided line, plus a three-way swivel with a round 1½oz lead ball attached via a snap link. On the business end was a 10-foot 20lb test mono trace sporting a size 2 hook, with a small glo-bead threaded on above. To the hook an inch of orange wool was added completing what, to me at least, seemed a rather strange combination.

Below *Tour operator Christine Slater, of Tailor Made Holidays, helps guide Greg Hunt display the shark-like appearance of her first white sturgeon, estimated at around 150lb. It was hooked in fifty feet of water from a narrow gorge along the Harrison River and jumped completely clear of the calm surface within twenty seconds of feeling cold steel. Note its fully protrusible vacuum-like mouth, used for hoovering up salmon eggs and even salmon carcasses from the rocky bottom.*

Above *The province of British Columbia is graced with some of the most fertile, fish-producing and stunningly beautiful rivers on our planet, most stacked with steep-sided hills full of cedar, pine, birch, hemlock and giant fir. This is the famous Copper River where I caught magnificent steelhead trout during the making of one of my international* Go Fishing *television programmes during the early 1990s.*

Christine, Andy and I donned neoprene chest waders, provided by Greg, and positioned ourselves two yards out and about 40 yards apart, making casts of the same length directly out. The lead ball then bounced gently downstream and across (hence the term 'bottom bouncing') from pebble to pebble pulling the fly and bead combination behind it across the current in similar fashion to presenting the wet fly in downstream-and-across mode with a fast sinking line. The secret to interpreting bites comes from watching the 'tap, tap, tap' of the rod tip as the lead plinks over the gravel, and striking when it pauses momentarily or does something unusual. It is in fact a most fascinating technique (that we enjoyed for at least a couple of hours each day) and similar to one I used several years back when fishing Sweden's famous Morrum River for sea trout and salmon, except that then we used 4-inch long ½-inch diameter lead-filled plastic tubes (to avoid snagging on the rocky riverbed) and large tube flies instead of a glo bead/corkie/hook-wool combo. I did in fact switch over to standard dressed size 4 and 2 British salmon flies, and still caught well. There were so many fish in the river running upstream in waves that there was little point in casting and wading downstream a yard before casting again, as we would when covering an entire pool for Atlantic salmon. With the potential of five separate species both fresh run and dark, all moving through the same run, hook-ups were commonplace and whilst I am sure everyone would prefer to land silver-sided fish fresh in from the sea, Canadian anglers enjoy the ensuing battle with 'whatever' coloured fish they catch.

The first cock chum salmon I hooked into, for instance, was getting on for 30lb, almost in full spawning dress, yet it almost spooled me before Greg saw my plight and brought the boat over. We finally beached it on the opposite bank some half a mile downstream, such is the speed of flow in this incredible river. Chum salmon do in fact start to colour up very quickly upon entering freshwater and whilst we did take a few silver beauties with sea lice still attached, most were easily distinguishable from chinooks (which were equally thick on the ground) by their dark vertical bars along the flanks and deeply forked tail, the chinook's tail being spade-like. To obtain even more enjoyment from these unbelievable runs of salmon in both the Fraser and Harrison rivers, which also included small concentrations of cohos most of which were silver, I put up my 10-foot 'Heritage' single-handed saltwater fly rod and size 9 lead cored line with a size 4 salmon fly on the 12lb test leader – and didn't I have to start running quickly downriver to keep up with both chums and chinooks of 20lb plus. It was simply marvellous fishing. How often, for instance, do you lose count of the salmon you catch in a week's fishing, with half of the week spent sturgeon fishing at anchor anyway. British Columbia certainly provides men with dreams to dream, just like the song.

On one particularly grey and rainy morning before we started sturgeon fishing, our guide, Danny Hartland, suggested we try a spot of bar fishing for chinooks. Bar fishing is something different again, and can only be described as a mixture of lure fishing and uptiding. The boat is anchored in really shallow water on a gravel bar close to the shoreline (hence the terminology) and three or four rods are put out over the opposite side with heavy leads. To a wire boom secured immediately above the lead a 4-foot mono trace is added to present the unlikely combination of a size 2/0 single unbaited hook above which is a fluorescent coloured spin-n-glo (a 1-inch-diameter egg-shaped cork ball fitted with two propellers). It was the first time I had ever ledgered a lure, but the rig certainly works by spinning away down there close to the bottom and is attacked, by chinook salmon in particular, in a most aggressive manner as they run upriver fresh in from the Pacific Ocean. Suddenly one of the rods, which are all bent over by water pressure, springs back alarmingly and there on the end is a salmon – though you must be quick reeling in the now-slack line (just like when uptiding) before striking into the salmon. I can't say it's the most challenging technique I've ever used but my first fish was a fresh-run silver chinook of about 10lb. Had it been a monster of 40-50lb plus, which during the months of June and July are considered everyday catches, then I guess bar fishing would now be topping Wilson's favourite method list.

Interspersed with sturgeon sessions we sampled the salmon fishing at several locations in both rivers. The hottest spot by far was a long, fast run immediately below huge rafts of cut logs (waiting for higher water to be taken downstream by tug) at the mouth of where the Harrison joins the Fraser. It is a very popular spot with local anglers, and each time we fished there or passed by, someone's rod was bent over by a big chinook or chum salmon. We had some great fun float fishing there too, using a clump of fresh salmon eggs on the hook – trotting the bait down using a small multiplier and 20lb braid proved a real winner for both tackle control and striking. Replacing the eggs on the float set-up with a single-hook fly spoon (called a Colorado locally) was also

Previous spread *A high, Polaris-style leap is generally not what anglers expect from fish hooked on the river bed. But each and every white sturgeon obliges in spectacular fashion. Sometimes immediately, but more commonly at the end of its long initial run like this near-200 pounder hooked by Christine Slater.*

Right *Using an ultra-light spinning outfit and small spoon, this silver-sided 7lb coho salmon put up a tremendous scrap. They are highly prized by local anglers and average 5–8 lb. Favourite haunts are shallow sloughs behind the shoreline connected to the river by narrow riffles.*

an effective salmon producer. Yes, I know trotting a spinner downstream appears certifiable, but believe me it works.

With another guide, Tony Nootebos, we also explored some of the shallow sloughs behind the shoreline connected to the river by narrow riffles. Cohos were the target species here and we caught some super silver fish to 7-8lb using ultra-light spinning gear and small single-hook spoons. The same technique also worked in the narrow Vedder River which merges with the Fraser downstream of Island 22, our launching site. As expected, however, there wasn't enough time in just six days even to scratch the surface of this unique watershed. So we shall just have to return again and again. Had we stuck purely to fishing for sturgeon (with up to ten or more hits in an afternoon session) the chances of a real whopper turning up would have been doubled, although the best of the week caught by Christine, measuring over 7 feet long, with an estimated weight of 200lb plus certainly exceeded our expectations. So anyone bent on putting their name on one is best advised to visit at peak time between August and November. December and January however, though colder (British Columbia has a similar climate to the UK), still produce numbers of this truly fascinating and ancient species. As Vancouver is just a 9½-hourhour flight away from Heathrow, the trip is well worthwhile.

NAMIBIA'S SKELETON COAST
AFRICA

Namibia's famous Skeleton Coast (so named from the numbers of boats that have run aground on the reefs) in South West Africa is the shore-fisherman's fantasy land. It stretches north for nearly 1,000 miles between South Africa and the Angolan border. Here you will find beach fishing the like of which you have never experienced before and unquestionably the most thrilling, back-breaking, awesome stand-up saltwater sportsfishing you have ever encountered in your lifetime.

The 30lb monofilament reel line has already stretched to its limit and is as tight as a bowstring, singing in the wind like a canary. My powerful 14½-foot carbon beachcaster can bend no further. With both heels dug deeply into the golden sand, legs bent almost to a squat in order to lower my centre of gravity and my aching spine arched back past the vertical, I am literally leaning my entire weight against the unseen, immovable force hugging the reef over 200 yards beyond the surf. Yet still the bronze whaler shark, my third of the afternoon session, will not yield and continues to rip line at will from the multiplier in long, powerful surges, over an hour from when it was first hooked.

I am in Namibia. The rich inshore waters are crammed full of pilchards and mullet at the bottom end of the food chain, with guitar fish, catfish, steenbras (a thickset bream-like fish with a piggish snout which reaches weights in excess of 40lb), kob and various rays plus spotted gully sharks and hound sharks in the middle providing a veritable banquet for the largest sharks at the very top of the chain. Most common is the incredible bronze whaler (*Carcharhinus brachyurus*) which is present in vast numbers between 100lb and 300lb (the South African record is over 400lb) and the cow shark which reaches weights of 150–200lb. The latter, however, cannot hold a candle to the speed and sheer stamina of the bronze whaler, also called copper shark due to the coppery sheen which extends along the back and sides of its long and athletic body. Though occasionally found in deep water, the bronze whaler favours temperate to cool, shallow water, which is probably why it concentrates in such phenomenal numbers along the Skeleton Coast of Namibia. For anyone wishing to experience big fish in the surf, Namibia has no equal. There are, of course, other types of safaris to enjoy. The country is rich in wildlife and organized big game viewing, shooting and photographic trips are extremely popular. But fishermen visit Namibia for only one reason – to fight stand-up battles with bronze whalers.

Long-haul flights land only at Windhoek, the capital of Namibia, after which it is a four-hour drive to the coastal town of Swakopmund. Many of the local guides are based here and will pick you up from your hotel in a four-wheel drive vehicle completely kitted out with one-piece 14-foot South African-style surf rods and multipliers, plus terminal rigs and fresh bait. I met one such guide a few years back, Ottmar Leippert, a German, who runs Levo Sportsfishing Safaris from Walvis Bay which is just a few miles south of Swakopmund, and we have been firm friends ever since. I was on a reconnaissance trip at the time with Christine Slater of Tailor Made Holidays to the upper reaches of the Zambezi River along the Zambian–Namibian border in search of tiger fish, and we stopped in Swakopmund *en route*. Unfortunately it was in July, their winter, with little chance of bronze whalers. We did catch several spotted gully and hound sharks however, and I was impressed enough to return. Moreover Ottmar guaranteed that when I returned with a party of guests the following February, everyone would have more than their fill of fighting bronzes, as he calls them. And he was right. The best window for bronze whaler action is between January and April, although there is a wealth of other species to catch all year round.

What many newcomers to Namibian sharking have trouble comprehending when they first catch 20-40lb hound or spotted gully sharks, any one of which would have fellow anglers crowding around on a British beach, is that locally these small sharks are simply considered bait. To set out a chum line the small shark is slit from throat to vent and staked in the sand so the waves recede carrying a blood trail. On some days this attracts bronze whalers so quickly that sets of dorsal and tail fins can be seen in the rollers, working back and forth parallel to the beach within minutes. I've even seen bronze whalers rush in on a wave and grab hold of their staked-out brethren.

At this point baiting up with the smaller sharks' gills, which are full of blood, initiates a hit within seconds of it settling on the bottom less than a cricket wicket length out.

It is the bait *par excellence*. For ease of casting, however, smallish baits such as mullet and mackerel heads or chunks are supplied by the guide. Generally a cast of between just 50 and 100 yards will put the bait beyond the breakers into a depth where the bronzes are working. Even such short distances however are not easily accomplished without first practising using the rod and reel combination required to land these sharks. All Namibian and South African surf casters fish with the reel at the bottom of their powerful 14-foot rods, leaving just enough grip below for the left hand to thumb the spool during casting. You simply have to learn to cast in this way (though your guide will oblige if required) because it is impossible to play a shark with the reel fixed anywhere but low down. Two-hour fights are commonplace and there is no way anyone's back could stand the pressure of reeling in with the reel set high up.

Most Namibian guides use multipliers that can comfortably hold over 300 yards of 35lb test, Penn's GLS25 and the Daiwa Sealine series being most popular. To maximize

Above *No wonder this South African angler has an ear-to ear-grin. His prize is a 55lb kob, known locally as kabeijou, caught from the surf whilst shark fishing. These highly prized bass-like fish have been known to reach weights in excess of 100lb, although ten- to twenty-five-pounders are the general run. They will occasionally snap up a mullet or mackerel head or fillet but show a distinct preference for small livebaits or small whole squid.*

on casting potential I decided to use my old faithful ABU 10000 and loaded it to the brim with just 30lb test. I must admit to coming close a few times, even with well over 300 yards on board, but I was never spooled. The rod I used was made up for me specially by Terry Carrol of ZZiplex. I always like using my own gear when abroad and though two piece, this powerful 14½-footer comprising a 6½-foot butt and 8-foot tip more than fitted the bill with sharks to 240lb.

The secret to the reasonably long casting of large, non-aerodynamic baits such as a mullet or mackerel head is using an uncomplicated terminal set-up. To the reel line a 20-foot 100lb test rubbing trace is joined (using the beachcasting knot) and for fishing specifically over sand, a sliding lead link with cushioning bead above a 9/0 hook trace made from 20 inches of 150lb nylon covered wire, the 4–6oz bomb being joined to the link with 20 inches of 40lb test. This seems to cast better, rather than clipping the bomb directly to the sliding lead link. For rocky bottoms a fixed lead also on a 20-inch 'rotten bottom' mono link (in case it becomes snagged in the rocks) is simply tied to the top of the hook trace swivel. And that's it. Generally speaking it is not difficult to hook into a bronze whaler. The real expertise lies with your guide in choosing the right location on the day from anywhere along the 200 miles of shoreline. I've known Ottmar drive for miles first to one spot and then another, studying the tide, weed build-ups, the sea's colour, wave formations and so on. He dislikes brown or dirty water, and I'm sure the bronzes do too. So he'll sit there with the engine of his Land Rover switched off for several minutes, sniffing the wind direction with eyes glued to the water, before stopping or moving quickly on! Ottmar knows all the beaches intimately both south and north of Swakopmund and when conditions seem right he thinks nothing of driving distances of up to 100 miles in order to put his guests quickly on to bronzes. I share his sentiments entirely and would always rather drive for two hours, perhaps fish successfully for six and then drive home again, than stand there fishless and bored out of my skull for ten hours.

One of the most enchanting locations favoured by Ottmar is south of Walvis Bay, all the way around Pelican Point to Donkey Bay. Here flocks of flamingos can be seen sifting mud in shallow lagoons built from land reclamation and in the bay itself fishermen share sandy beaches with huge concentrations of fur seals. Often a group will swim by for a friendly look-see just a few yards out and occasionally touch your line. There are in fact some 200,000 fur seals along the 100-mile length of coastline immediately north of Swakopmund and the number inhabiting the entire Namibian coastline from South Africa to Angola totals a staggering 1.4 million. You can thus appreciate the numbers of fish that must be present in these waters just to sustain them let alone the massive concentrations of sharks. The downside for the seals however is the processing factory which handles 35,000 culled animals annually for the manufacture of seal-fur shoes, with the meat going to Africa's interior for human consumption. It does seem a heartless world at times, especially when every so often a young seal separated from its mother will leave the surf and come flapping across the beach for a free offering of mullet or mackerel from your hand – a wonderful experience.

Those like me who consider that cormorants are largely responsible for the demise of silver shoal species in many of our British inland waterways, will no doubt be interested in the cormorant populations around Swakopmund. There is, for instance, a 17,000 square metre platform half a mile offshore just south of the town which was constructed during the 1930s specifically for gathering the excreta of cormorants. Back in 1938 statistics record that 900,000 birds used the platform to roost. Today the platform attracts 350,000 birds each night. The resulting guano, used for fertiliser, is collected anually and amounts to 900 tons. That's an awful lot of dead pilchards and mullet.

Even without the attraction of a blood trail provided by a slit, staked-out small shark or rubby-dubby bag full of mashed up mullet or mackerel, if there are any bronzes around they are invariably quickly on to your bait. Sometimes there is an initial knock as the rod tip is pulled down abruptly when the shark moves off on the lookout for

Above *Huge colonies of fur seals are to be found along the Skeleton Coast around the old German settlement town of Swakopmund. They are extremely inquisitive and often swim under and around the line actually plucking it with their flippers, but a shark angler soon becomes accustomed to such 'line bites'. There is never any doubt when a bronze whaler grabs the bait and slams the rod down hard.*
Next spread *My son Lee helps display the largest bronze whaler I*

*caught during a week's fishing.
Estimated with a weight-for-length
system used by all the Namibian
guides (such fish are impossible to
weigh with scales on the beach), this
superb specimen was around 240lb. It
certainly pulled my string for almost
two hours and made me sweat like I
never have before. Note its huge
powerful fins, athletic lines and
distinctly bronze-grey back. A stretchy
50lb test monofilament reel line can
certainly do wonderful things.*

another titbit. At this point it is best to lower the rod and wait until the line is pulled completely tight before heaving the rod back and yanking it hard a few times to ensure a firm hook-up. Incidentally whilst most fishermen like to leave their rods in rests whilst waiting for a run, I much prefer to hold mine throughout. I've seen too many rods suddenly catapult from the rest and go sliding through the sand towards the surf – usually followed by the owner sprinting as fast as his legs will go. If all goes according to plan after hooking up, your shark heads off for the horizon through the rollers and you watch in amazement as line evaporates from the reel despite a firmly set clutch. It's then a case of tightening up even more at each new surge from the shark, slowing it down gradually over a distance of between 200 and 300 yards if it's a sizeable specimen of 200lb or more.

Brute force simply cuts no ice with bronze whalers as they are too strong by far. However once you have played and landed a few, working your fish becomes second nature.

It is useless for instance simply standing still and expecting to pump the shark in as though you were boat fishing. Torque on your tackle is so great that only small fish can be landed successfully in this way. It is far better to clamp down on the spool at the end of a run when the shark has slowed down and walk backwards up the beach using the full power of the rod and fully stretched line together in horsing it towards the shore. To recover line you then run down the beach winding like a madman until the shark realizes what's happening and decides to make yet another long, sickening run. Sickening because all your hard work suddenly seems in vain as 100 yards of line leave the reel and you're back to square one again! Many anglers like to take a breather or two during the fight and relieve the pressure on their spine by sitting down in the sand and just holding on. I must admit to doing this once during the fight of a big fish foul-hooked in one of its huge pectoral fins, a fish that I simply couldn't budge despite maximum pressure. The trouble with relaxing yourself however is that you also give the shark a breather and so ultimately it will then take longer to subdue. But if you keep your head and continue to work the shark by moving back up and then down the beach, you'll eventually get to see its dorsal and upper tail lobe cutting through the breakers – a truly wonderful sight. But if it's a big fish in a tidy sea with a strong undertow you could still have half an hour or more before it's finally lying at your feet on the sand. To get it there your guide must leap into the waves with a long-handed gaff and find purchase in the shark's dorsal fin root (less harm is done than jaw gaffing) before hauling on the trace and crabbing it to shore, which is always easier said than done. There is then plenty of time to unhook your prize and secure the event on film before dragging it back to the breakers and watching the two fins eventually disappear from view. Only bronze hooks are used incidentally, never stainless steel in case the trace has to be cut on a deeply hooked shark. Its powerful digestive juices will then rust the hook away to nothing.

Unfortunately not all hook-ups result in a shark on the beach. I've had the hook suddenly pull free (it was obviously not set from the start), even after playing fish for as long as an hour or more, and experienced the line suddenly parting across rocks at various stages of the fight. Even more frustrating, and on one particular occasion this happened to me on no fewer than three consecutive casts, the line above the trace is bitten through by the cruising sharks with their mouths open, nowhere near the bait. You feel a gentle knock on the rod tip, followed a second later by the line falling completely slack, and when you reel in it has been heavily serrated by their long, triangular razor-sharp teeth. The only remedy is to make a much shorter cast once you have tackled up again. Even then fish working through the second or third breakers as they regularly do are quite capable of repeating the problem. On more than one occasion whilst standing thigh deep and waiting for a bite, I've looked along the surf and seen sets of fins little further out than myself – which is quite a sobering sight I can tell you.

When you finally start to get the better of fish which have throughout the fight fought way, way out, they will often kite along the beach one way or the other. The tempting option here is to run along the beach with them, and if their route passes over known reefs you just have to follow and keep the line well up so as not to break off. But with those that veer shorewards over clean sand it's best to stay put, because once the shark reaches shallow water over sand it will kite back out again and towards you providing the pressure is kept on. What complicates this routine is when several anglers are all fishing in close proximity and everyone hooks up, which is a common occurrence. Then all hell breaks loose. I can vividly remember a particular trip shared with my son, Lee, and two nephews, Martin and Richard Bowler and two other friends, when exactly this occurred. Ottmar had driven us north to one of his favourite bronze whaler marks at a location called Mile 100 – which is exactly 100 miles from Swakopmund. And literally within ten minutes of casting out our mullet heads, all six of us were into fish. It was quite unbelievable and a case of running deftly along the beach lifting the line above or below the next man's rod to keep them apart until each shark had headed way out in a different direction and settled down. Fortunately Ottmar had organized his friend and fellow guide Neil Van Rooyen to come along and help with the landing, otherwise we'd have been in a right pickle.

The longest fight any of us experienced took three hours and almost had nephew Richard completely exhausted. All bronze battles with fish over 150lb will include a pain barrier at some period when you start to wish you'd never hooked the shark in the first place. The pressure on your arms and back is enormous. Richard's problem with this particular bronze however which, when finally landed over half a mile from where it picked up his bait, weighed over 200lb, was that he had to endure three hours of torture from badly sunburned feet, which were badly swollen, bright pink and covered in large yellow blisters following his very first afternoon on the beach. To play a big shark for that length of time must have been excruciatingly painful but I take my hat off to him, there was no way he was going to hand that rod over.

For those wishing to scale down their tackle to monofilament traces, smaller hooks and small whole fresh fish or fish strip there are a dozen or more exciting species just waiting to grab hold. Guitar fish averaging 5-10lb called sand sharks (a local name) are commonplace as are small catfish which at times can prove a real nuisance even to shark baits. Stringrays are also likely customers, in particular the blue stingray and the eagle ray which has pointed wings and a bulbous, raised head. The two most highly prized species locally both for their fighting and eating qualities are the steenbras and the kob. There are in fact six separate species of kob found off the southern African coastline, the largest reaching weights of 150lb. I have caught this superb bass-like fish, although I'm never sure which species is which, in several countries around the world. In Morocco it is called corbine, in The Gambia they call it cassarva and in

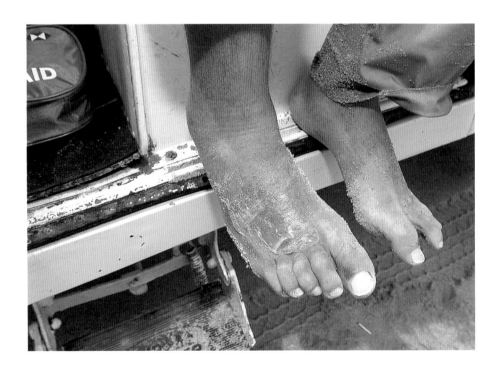

Above *I don't know whether our guide, Ottmar, is hard up for hooks or just plain barmy. This 150lb bronze whaler was still very much alive and swam off strongly once Ottmar had retrieved the size 9/0. He certainly has a way with sharks and his comical, often outrageous, actions kept our party entertained all week.*

Left *Not a pretty sight and a testament to the strength of ultraviolet rays. Even during low cloud and drizzle along the Skeleton Coast severe sunburn can occur. These blistered porkies belong to my nephew Richard Bowler from Dunstable. Enough said.*

Next spread *Wildlife and* *organized game viewing, shooting and photographic safaris are extremely popular in Namibia. There are in fact over twenty national parks and game reserves covering 15 per cent of the country's area. In the remote mountainous desert of the north-west roam the last free-ranging desert rhino in the world, and with them the uniquely adapted desert elephant, still following ancient migration routes. Namibia also has the world's largest population of cheetahs, 90 per cent of which actually live outside the proclaimed conservation areas.*

Australia it is given the name of jewfish. The most distinctive feature common to all those I've caught is a yellowy orange stain inside the mouth. Its local name in Namibia is kabeijou and at certain times of the year it is present in vast shoals. I've enjoyed some hectic sport with kabeijou in the 3-6lb range whilst fishing offshore from Swakopmund on Ottmar's 20-foot ski boat, and although I have seen whoppers to over 50lb caught from the surf on baits intended for sharks, I personally have still yet to catch a big one. But I'll be back.

THE CAUVERY RIVER
SOUTH INDIA

E ven at 1,261,813 square miles, India is only one-third the area of China in land mass, yet her 940 million people amount to five-sixths of China's population. India is the most over-populated country on this planet, where, as in all Third World countries, first and foremost fish are food. Quality sportsfishing is available in some isolated protected locations both in the extreme north and in south India, where the mighty mahseer still rules.

During the past 50 years however indiscriminate dynamiting, poaching and netting of most major mahseer-holding river systems, plus the creation of large dams and hydroelectric plants, have all taken their toll by greatly reducing stocks and the mahseer's natural habitat of fast-flowing rocky rivers. However there are isolated locations that still provide quality fishing. One such southern river is the famous Cauvery (pronounced and sometimes spelt Kaveri) which rises close to the Kerala border at Madikeri some 80 miles due west of Mysore, famous for its sandlewood. North of the city the Cauvery becomes the massive Krishnavaja Sagara Dam (named after a maharaja of Mysore in the 1920s) before heading in an easterly direction through dense jungles, flowing to within 60 miles south of Bangalore, known as the garden city capital of Karnataka state. It then enters the state of Tamil Nadu and continues flowing in an easterly direction all the way to Chibambaran (a total distance of 475 miles) where it empties into the Indian Ocean via an enormous delta. *En route* there is a spectacularly beautiful and remote section of

Previous spread *Taking in the stark, raw beauty of the game- and mahseer-rich Cauvery Valley, as I am doing here immediately above the falls at Meke-Datu in the state of Karnataka, I could easily be back in Norfolk looking out across my own two lakes. For I love both locations with equal passion and consider both as home.*

Above *Mahseer fishing is like no other. From a narrow torrent within a chasm contorted by the force of powerful currents over thousands of years, Andy Davison relies upon the combined skills of our faithful friends and river guides, Suban and Bola, to extract a big mahseer. A fish which is still nowhere near finished, despite having dragged the trio down river across hot rock for over 400 yards, and which will continue to fight every inch of the way until totally exhausted.*

the Cauvery, south of Bangalore, exquisitely diverse in flora and fauna, where even 100lb monster mahseer are still an attainable goal.

In fact the river below Sirasmundram is a curious natural phenomenon. It flows off the Deccan Plateau at the Gaganachucki and Barachucki waterfalls which drop over 300 feet, forming a natural barrier against any fish trying to migrate further upstream. Around 25-30 miles down river at Meke–datu is another extremely high set of falls, also impassable, which traps the mahseer between these two points. The rugged and hostile wilderness within the surrounding countryside of deep, rocky gorges and impenetrable thorn scrub jungle provides daily sightings of elephant, wild boar, deer, jackals, monkeys, black bear, russel vipers and cobras, maybe even the occasional panther (the Indian name for leopard). There is a formidable galaxy of colourful birds too, including kingfishers, drongoes, pea fowl, jungle fowl, paradise flycatchers, woodpeckers, bulbuls, mynahs, parakeets, bee eaters, golden orioles and hornbills, as well as several birds of

prey such as fish eagles, kites, ospreys and vultures keeping a watchful eye on the river from above. Containing families of ever-playful otters and more large (mugger) crocodiles than are ever seen elsewhere, this part of the Cauvery River is one of the most fascinating spots on earth beside which to camp out safari-style beneath the stars, whether you are woken abruptly at dawn to the spine-chilling bellow of a bull elephant or merely sit and revel in the total silence. We Westerners think we know what silence is yet planes overhead, distant tractors on the land or simply the voices of other people never leave us. None are evident along the Cauvery Valley. It is my very favourite place of all.

The river's rich, green floodplain, totally submerged by the monsoon rains from June to October, can measure up to 500 yards across between tall hills burnt brown by the sun. Then just around the next bend the Cauvery will drastically narrow into 'boiling' water through a steep gorge, providing perfect mahseer living conditions (although some are caught from slower pools) of white cascading rapids flowing at up to ten knots around a twisting maze of black bedrock. This is unquestionably amongst the most challenging, difficult pieces of river any angler is ever likely to experience – and this is why great fish still exist here. As important however is the fact that much of the fishing within this veritable mahseer haven, where for some 15 years now I have experienced many a memorable battle and made wonderful friends, is under strict control. The sportsfishing is managed jointly by Jungle Lodges and Resorts and by the Wildlife

Above *Surely there are few more exciting moments than this. My wife, Jo, Bola and I had not been perched on 'centre rock' (one of my favourite big mahseer runs) for more than ten minutes when a family of elephants came down to drink. Sharing their world and that of all the other creatures in the valley from otters at play to fish eagles soaring high overhead, with a very real chance of coming to grips with the world's most mesmeric freshwater fish, is what year after year takes me back to the heat, the beauty and the stark contrasts of India.*

J. DeWet Van Ingens' 120 lber taken on the 22nd March 1946.

Above *Using what we would now class as ancient tackle, this 120lb world-record golden mahseer was caught on a four-inch spoon from the Kabbini, a tributary of the mighty Cauvery, by the late J. DeWet Van Ingen nearly sixty years ago. Oh, what marvellous fishing existed in those days, when big mahseer were the prized quarry of viceroys, princes, kings and maharajahs alike.*

Association of South India, which was formed in 1972 (and of which I am proud to be a life member), who employ year-round guards to minimize illegal poaching and dynamiting.

During the Raj, the British rule which ended in 1947, many rivers throughout India were full of Carnatic carp and mahseer. The world-renowned Hardy Brothers of Alnwick specialized in rods, reels, lines, artificial lures and flies for India. Three-piece 16-foot steel-centred built cane and green heart rods with two fly and one spinning top joint, and Silex centrepin reels, were what every army officer of the day used to

Left A thickset golden mahseer of around 40lb, now almost spent, is eased slowly upstream against the fierce current by one of southern India's most accomplished hunting and fishing ladies, Dr Nanda Subbanna, following a titanic battle lasting over half an hour. Now fully 150 yards downstream from where it was first hooked, the faithful guide, Suban, can start thinking about lifting it out in his arms and removing the 6/0 hook before returning it to the Cauvery River.

combat the might and devastatingly long runs of the mahseer. Monofilament lines, of course, were yet to be invented so the mahseer angler at the beginning of the twentieth century made do with dressed silk or hard-braided tanned flax lines to which a loop end of twisted best gut was spliced for attaching a 12-20-inch gut cast for the hook or lure. Those were the days. I cannot imagine however playing a big mahseer in fast, rocky rapids on anything less than forgiving 40lb test monofilament completely filling a smooth-running multiplier (the ABU 10000 is perfect) coupled to an 11-foot fast taper, hollow-glass bass or uptide rod. But our forefathers did it.

It is all a far cry from those early times during the Raj when books by Thomas, Skene Dhu and Jim Corbett inspired British Army anglers into packing their tackle. Catches of 20, 30, even 50 mahseer, albeit of mainly modest size fish, being caught in a day by a couple of rods and mostly on lures too, were not unusual. The mighty mahseer became the prized quarry of viceroys, princes, kings and maharajahs alike. The Prince of Wales (later Edward VIII), for instance, fished near Mysore for mahseer in 1922, guided by the Van Ingens.

The specific identities of the Indian large-scale carps (for the mahseer is indeed a cyprinid possessing larger pharyngeal teeth size for size than any other) has always been a confusing subject. The overall Latin name adopted is *Barbus tor* indicating that the mahseer is more barbel-like than any other member of the carp family. There are however considered to be no fewer than six separate species of mahseer, four of which are confined to the northern Indian rivers and those of Burma, and two in the south of India. The first, which grows the largest by far, is *Barbus tor* 'Mussellah' (Sykes), also known as the hump-backed mahseer and the species we modern anglers lovingly refer to as the golden mahseer. Incidentally the world record for the golden mahseer, weighing 120lb, was caught on a four-inch spoon by the late J. De Wet Van Ingen (one of the famous taxidermy brothers from Mysore) from the upper reaches of the Kabbini River (a tributary of the Cauvery) on 22 March 1946. There is also a black mahseer, a melanistic form of the above species and not separate. The second southern species *Barbus tor* 'Khundree' (Sykes), sometimes called the Deccan mahseer, is a noticeably slimmer fish and completely silvery in coloration in both body and fins, whereas the fins of the golden mahseer are orangey.

All mahseer are equipped with huge mouths, rimmed by exceptionally thick lips plus two short and two very long barbels for probing beneath and between rocks for their staple diet of small fishes and river crabs. Mahseer are totally omnivorous however and in addition to a rubbery paste called ragi (millet flour, boiled to bring out the gluten so it stays on the hook) they will also hit artificial lures and greedily hoover up worms, frogs and flies. Common to many mahseer (though not all) are their strange hypertrophied lips, a pronounced adipose extension. The mahseer's most striking features however are its disproportionately large, powerful fins and its armour-like scales. This fish has by far the largest scales to be found on any freshwater species, and it is customary, should one unfortunately become dislodged (as with tarpon), to press it flat between the pages of a heavy book and record upon it in ink the fish's weight and date of capture.

Of course there are numerous other weird and wonderfully shaped and coloured species in the Cauvery including several types of catfish (some quite large), Carnatic carp, red carp, pink carp (similar to our barbel), murrel, and dozens of lesser varieties whose names I don't know. Using a heavy feeder rod or a light carp rod and 10lb line you could (and I have) enjoy sport all day long using ledgered worms or small pieces of ragi paste – until, that is, you hook a truck belting down the motorway at 60 miles per hour on totally inadequate tackle. The mahseer certainly rules but can only be pursued seriously between the months of January and April when water levels have drastically

Above *Monstrous golden mahseer, like this hump-backed immensely thick-set 91 pounder, represent the ultimate in trophy shots. Following an hour's strength-sapping battle in which guide Suban and I risked life and limb in our efforts to extract it from a set of rapids over a quarter of a*

mile in length, and it covered every holding pool from top to bottom, such was my adrenaline rush that I could still muster a smile for the camera. The successful bait was a 1lb 8oz livebait cast upstream through a mixture of white water and car-sized boulders, and worked back down again.

Above *If there is a factor common to all young children in Third World countries, despite their meagre surroundings, it is that they are always smiling and happy with their lot. This group come from the small village in Sangam where our guides, Bola and Suban, live, just above the Cauvery flood plain.*

receded from the previous summer's monsoon flooding and mahseer holding areas and pools can be defined.

Now although spoons and plugs will produce on the day (low water levels are best) they are, overall, difficult to work within the river's terrain of confined pools and unbelievably uneven bottom strata of jagged black bedrock. Favoured mahseer baits along this section of the Cauvery are chicken egg-sized lumps of ragi paste, or chilwa, the name given to any 5- to 12-inch live or freshly killed fish regardless of species, and river crabs.

By employing a two ounce coil of strip lead wound tightly around the line 12-18 inches above a strongly forged 6/0 hook (I prefer Drennan O'Shaunessey), a cast is made diagonally downstream and across, starting from the top of each pool or run with a view to deliberately (I know it seems mad) snagging the lead amongst the rocks. Currents where the largest mahseer reside are so fierce, even a 2lb boat lead would not hold bottom. Yet when a mahseer extends its protrusile mouth around the bait and hoovers it up, the lead coil is instantly pulled free. Most bites feel literally as though your line has been tied to the tailboard of a juggernaut, which is one reason for always holding on to your rod and keeping the tip up high to minimize water pressure against the line. It is tiring, extremely demanding but utterly fascinating fishing.

When presenting chilwa, hooked just beneath the dorsal fin root, I often lob the bait well upstream and across, holding the rod up high, and slowly mend the line as the current bumps it downstream from rock to rock. Unbelievably savage bites are instigated by this technique, whether on the move or whilst waiting a while with the lead coil caught in a crevice. Being their natural food, chilwa often produces a big fish from a pool where ragi has failed. Crabs are equally successful. To mount, wind a few turns of 20lb monofilament tightly around the middle of the crab's carapace and tie off, before inserting the hook point beneath – so simple yet so effective. The beauty of ragi however is that previously unfished and unexplored areas can be prebaited with a couple of dozen balls every other day for a week, with an excellent chance of mahseer being caught as a result.

So what makes this particular fish to me and all those who have also endured memorable battles with leviathans in the 50-100lb bracket so emphatically special? Well, quite frankly, tarpon apart, I cannot think of another fresh- or saltwater creature owning scales and fins that could hold a candle to the awesome incredible power of the mahseer which just keeps on fighting to within a second of total exhaustion. In most battles your prize only comes to the surface at the very end to reveal its size, whereupon it can be secured using a soft rope stringer loop passed carefully through the cavernous mouth and out through a gill opening. The mahseer is then left tied to a marginal shrub to fully recover before releasing and taking any trophy shots. When its captor gently caresses the deep flanks of this mighty creature, you have what can only be described as the closest thing to a bond between man and fish. When landing such a monstrous fish, you feel physical pleasure, mental satisfaction and animal aggression. And when the fight is over and you return the gallant creature, there is compassion. No other fish within seconds of the hook finding purchase transforms a perfectly rational human being into a gibbering, frantic fighting machine with all regard for personal safety instantly abandoned. You are seized by an irresistible urge – wanting, praying and yearning to set eyes on the unseen force racking your body and tingling nerve ends like no fish ever managed to do before.

Enduring a stand-up encounter with a really big specimen, say a mahseer upwards of 70lb, guarantees you up to an hour or more of the most strength-sapping, gut-busting, arm-wrenching fight ever likely to be experienced in freshwater. Big mahseer almost always belt off downstream exactly like a barbel, often winding the line (which you can feel grating) between and around huge boulders. This is the reason why you need a 35-40lb reel line which could easily become shredded through bedrock to less than half its breaking strain. Because of this and the immense current forces involved, there is never any chance of playing a whopper back upstream to where it was first hooked. You are always obliged to go downriver following each long run, opposite to where the fish has decided to lie up, usually immediately behind a large boulder in order to apply direct pressure again. You must continue to follow its route downstream for as long as it takes – 200 yards, 500 yards, 1,000 yards or more, it matters not. Between times, of course, the mahseer has benefited from taking a breather while the angler becomes progressively more knackered through clambering over exposed bedrock and

Previous spread *Three people who have influenced my life so much during the past two decades, Bola, my wife, Jo, and Suban, display the golden fruits of what the Cauvery River is capable of bestowing upon fortunate anglers in a morning's fishing. An eighty-two-pounder for me and a forty-five-pounder for Jo. No wonder she looks tired. This marvellous brace came from adjoining pools below the rapids near a village called Haira where we love to camp beside the river. Jo's came to a ball of ragi and mine a 1lb-plus deadbait.*
Right *Mahseer have the largest scales of all freshwater fishes. Some are the size of beer mats. It is customary, should one unfortunately become dislodged (as with tarpon), to press it flat between the pages of a heavy book and record upon it in Indian ink (no pun intended) the fish's weight and date of capture. Andy Davison caught this sixty-pounder from the wide, steady water below crocodile rocks at Gali Bora using ragi paste.*

coarse marginal grasses, though the water itself, usually over 80 degrees Fahrenheit, is refreshingly pleasant in the intense heat of the river valley. At any time the guide might bundle you into a bamboo hide-covered coracle to follow the leviathan down the rapids through a chasm of foam and car-sized rocks, or to avoid parting company with a particular fish you may even choose to swim across the river itself in order to exert pressure from a different angle, as I have been obliged to do (or lose the fish) on several memorable occasions. Yes, part of mahseer magic is the opportunity for near 60 year-olds like me to become a boy again, and I shall hate the day when I can't.

ISLAMORADA, FLORIDA KEYS
UNITED STATES

The word 'keys' (or 'cays', as they are called in The Bahamas) simply means 'islands'. The Florida Keys consists of a chain of small islands extending south-west for over 100 miles to the southernmost point of the country. Numerous narrow strips of land and keys are joined together with bridges (43 in all) carrying Highway U.S.1. Arguably the largest and most productive saltwater angling location in the world, the Florida Keys offer diverse and exciting year-round sportsfishing in a tropical climate.

Reaching the Keys from the UK is relatively simple. Following a nine-hour flight to Miami International Airport from either Gatwick or Heathrow, you can hire a car and be halfway along the Keys within a couple of hours. Incidentally, whilst in Miami you could take in a trip to the famous Sea Aquarium and Parrot and Monkey Jungles, or visit the Everglades which blend into the northern boundaries and the start of the Florida Keys. Here Everglades ecotour adventures, airboat excursions, plus snake and alligator shows are daily features in what has been aptly described as Florida's 'wet prairie'. But let's continue south-west along Highway U.S.1 to the Keys, which are totally dedicated to the pursuits of sailing, scuba diving, sportsfishing and generally having a great time. Frankly I cannot think of anywhere else like it – unfortunately.

The entire eastern shoreline faces the deep blue Gulf Stream waters of the Atlantic Ocean where charter boats troll for the likes of billfish, cobia, wahoo, tuna and dorado, or drift over deep-water humps and wrecks for amberjacks, groupers or big sharks. On the quieter, western side are the shallow waters of Florida Bay, so completely different in character, where you can enjoy fishing 'back-country style' in a skiff (two anglers to a boat) poled along by an experienced guide through shallow reefs, around mangrove islands and across sandbars which offer spectacular light-tackle sport on both bait and fly for tarpon, snook, barracuda, permit, bonefish, jacks, redfish, spotted sea trout, ladyfish, sheepshead and many others. Angling ornithologists can also experience close encounters with pelicans, eagles, ospreys and myriad wading birds, and can admire the pink plumage of the unusual roseata spoonbill which roosts high in the mangrove tops. There are plenty of photo opportunities for the enthusiast. Many local anglers simply fish from the old road bridges or from the shore, and at times, particularly if wading for bonefish, there is good action to be had. But as the area of shoreline is so vast, varied and much affected by the height of the tides, the visitor is best advised to choose a location and book boat trips with experienced guides. My favourite spot is Islamorada, acclaimed – and justly so – as the 'sportsfishing capital of the world' which is roughly halfway down the Keys some 70 miles from Miami. To reach Islamorada you pass through Key Largo where memories of all those old black-and-white Humphrey Bogart movies come flooding back. In fact that's what I find most endearing about the Keys. It retains a distinct feel of Old America and visiting here is rather like going back in time.

As you arrive in Islamorada, which comprises Plantation Key, Windley Key, Upper and Lower Matecumbe Keys and Long Key, all connected together by several bridges for a total distance of some 26 miles, Whale Harbour Marina can be seen on the left. It is an excellent centre for booking charterboat trips out into the Atlantic or back-country skiff fishing. There is even a daily party boat trip where raw beginners can enjoy catching such fish as grunts and snappers. Incidentally, with regard to split charters, where perhaps one or two more people are required to make up a six-person blue-water trip, it pays to see the dockmaster at the marina. Islamorada offers a wide range of facilities including superb hotels and restaurants, dive centres, an underwater archaeological park, a Theatre of the Sea where you can even swim with the dolphins, plus truly huge bait and tackle shops. The Worldwide Sportsman, for instance, where

Previous spread *Jumping 100lb-plus tarpon in the dark or at first light using just a 20lb-class outfit is unbelievably exhilarating. Their sheer speed, agility and acrobatic skills are simply second to none. Which is why I personally never care if they come off, as indeed this particular fish did three leaps later. It's all part of the crazy world of tarpon fishing which, though a drug in itself, constitutes just a fraction of the unrivalled light-tackle tropical saltwater action on offer in the famous Florida Keys at the resort of Islamorada, considered by many to be the sportsfishing capital of the world.*

Right *Fancy experiencing the pain barrier? Then follow in the footsteps of my good mate Cambridgeshire angler Peter Hazlewood (left), and try fighting a big amberjack up on 50lb stand-up tackle from 300 feet down. This jumbo-sized specimen, held by Skipper Mike Groves, tipped the scales at 75lb. But I warn you, you'll not want to haul any more than a couple. Real headbangers will maybe go for three. Then it's back to the marina for spicy chicken wings, fried shrimp and a pitcher of beer. Yes, it sure is tough being an angling journalist.*

you can purchase anything from a designer 'flats shirt' to a complete saltwater fly-fishing or big-game trolling outfit, is so vast there is actually a full-size replica on the ground floor (which you can board) of Ernest Hemingway's famous fishing boat *Pilar*. And let's not forget that Islamorada is in fact the birthplace of all modern saltwater fly-fishing tackle and techniques. Such names as Jimmy Albright, Billy Pate, Billy Knowles, Joe Brooks and Lefty Kreh made it so with their catches of large bonefish, permit and tarpon on the fly. So the visiting fly rodder could not possibly choose a better saltwater destination.

At the lower end of the town as you leave, heading south towards Marathon (another great location), Bud 'n' Mary's renowned fishing marina is on the Atlantic side. Here you have a choice of heading into blue water after the whoppers on board an off-shore charter boat, joining a party boat trip, fishing with an experienced back-country guide from his 18-foot skiff (which includes the choice of both bait or fly-fishing tackle combos stored on board), or renting a skiff complete with live well and, with the aide of clearly marked maps, exploring yourself. The latter, however, particularly to the newcomer, although cheaper is rarely as productive as fishing with an experienced guide, who puts you straight on to fish. After all, that's what you're paying him for. Bud 'n' Mary's marina also has boat storage and servicing facilities for craft of up to 26 feet.

I first fished out of Islamorada in the early 1990s with my good friend Pete Hazlewood. In those days, along with two other mates, we were all more interested in the gut-busting action from lowering down a live bait like a grunt or blue runner and hauling up huge amberjacks from deep water on stand-up 50lb line class outfits. These unbelievable hard-battling jacks averaged between 50lb and 80lb and were present in astounding numbers over the Hump, a two-acre plateau of coral where the ocean floor rises steeply from 600 feet to just 300 feet deep, some 11 miles due east of Islamorada. We also trolled around the Hump and, on the way out, took black-fin tuna, barracudas and the stunningly coloured dorado. We also enjoyed battles with hammerhead sharks, or T-heads as they are more affectionately called in the Keys, which continually fed upon the amberjacks. Indeed, there were days when only three out of every four amberjacks hooked ever made it in one piece to the surface during the 20-minute fight, such was the ferocity of the hammerheads.

The amberjacks also had to withstand untold pressure from commercial fishing boats also working the Hump, who sold their hauls for, believe it or not, fertilizer. What a sad end to such a warrior of the deep – I can remember there and then thinking that nothing lasts for ever. Today, at certain times of the year, it is still worth trying for amberjacks over the Hump, but such has been the commercial rape of certain hot spots along the Keys that blue-water skippers are more likely to take those interested in drift fishing for jacks and groupers to secretly charted artificial reefs manufactured from old cars and tyres chained together. I guess it's fair and honest to say that, compared to just 20 or 30 years ago, sport is now nowhere near so prolific, but then on a global scale where and what is? We are all in some way or another to blame. Paradoxically the Florida Keys as a whole still truly rate at certain times of the year as a premier world-

wide sportsfishing destination. I certainly can't wait to get back again for my next tarpon trip – April through to June being the prime time.

I'd better explain here that gradually over the years as Pete and I revisited Islamorada, we became obsessed with the delights of back-country fishing. The chance of hooking a bonefish or even a permit on freelined shrimp using light to medium spinning tackle, or taking a bunch of lesser battlers, such as sheepshead or sea trout, on baited jigs became infinitely more desirable than hauling up jacks or sharks. So after just one day's heavy sport out in the Atlantic, in order to build up our muscles you understand, we then spent the remainder of our week in a skiff, two to a boat, hunting across the fascinatingly clear flats of Florida Bay. And our favourite target species by far was the acrobatic tarpon.

On one memorable occasion both Pete and I hooked and brought to the boat 100lb-plus tarpon before lunch using live mullet on float tackle. In the summer of 2000 it gave me immense pleasure to hand over a copy of my autobiography *Fifty Years a Fisherman* to our guide Lonny Shaw who still works out of Bud 'n' Mary's marina, knowing he would remember the photo that Pete took of him looking on as I played my tarpon. During that very same week in June 2000 I was with a party of eight Brits all bent on catching 100lb-plus tarpon from around the tidal channels passing through the bridges at Islamorada. Our guide was another old friend of mine, Essex skipper John Rawle, who from March through until the beginning of June each year runs specialized night-time trips starting at 3 a.m. and finishing at around 7.30 a.m. after tarpon, followed by several hours later if the guest fancies it, an afternoon's fun fishing for sharks on light tackle, plus the occasional permit, bonefish, jack or barracuda. Even at 3 a.m. the temperatures were a humid 80 degrees Fahrenheit and the shallow flats of Florida Bay ghostly calm as John twisted his 17-foot Maverick skiff, powered by a 115hp Yamaha at over 25 knots, around marker posts and through narrow mangrove channels, picking out landmarks every so often with a powerful spot lamp. I immediately noticed the strange sulphur-like aroma of the mangroves and also that because they hold moisture, air temperature close beside them was noticeably much, much cooler. When John finally cut the engine to set the skiff drifting slowly with the flow well downtide of a long road bridge in one of the main tarpon-running channels, two distinct sounds could be heard through the blackness: the occasional distant car or truck along Highway U.S.1 and the unmistakable sounds of huge tarpon crashing and feeding on the surface. It's a point worth mentioning here that tarpon usually move best with the tide when their shoals of prey fish are also on the move. Otherwise they tend to lay up between tides and wait, and are consequently more difficult to tempt. A 'busting' tarpon can sound as loud as a man jumping overboard (we're talking fish in the 80-200lb class here) or as muffled as someone popping a wine cork from a hundred yards away. It depends on how close you are to fish and how aggressively they are feeding on the night. Either way, expectations rise to fever pitch when the skiff is drifting amongst them with huge shapes rolling all around, as was the case on our first session during darkness.

In complete contrast to all my previous tarpon fishing in the Keys, which centred around daytime sessions, offering a float-fished live mullet, John Rawle much prefers the improved ratio of tarpon landed to those lost when using small blue crabs of 1½ to 3 inches across the carapace during the hours of darkness and at dawn. We caught the crabs the day before from grassy shallows around a mangrove island using hand nets, which was great fun in itself. To remove their pincers you simply grip each tightly with a pair of pliers. The crab will then automatically shed each limb as it does naturally when predated upon and will not die as a result. John keeps a good supply in a large wire mesh cage next to his tied-up skiff so fresh bait is always at hand. To present one on a size 5/0 'cutting-point' Owner hook, (model no. 5311), which is quite a small hook considering the tarpon's huge bony, fully-expandable jaws, a hole in one corner of the crab's shell is first made using an old hook, kept for that very purpose, sharpness being of paramount importance when seeking to maximize on tarpon hook-ups.

Right *Whether you choose to present shrimp on spinning tackle or drift the shallow flats with a fly rod, catching one of the world's top saltwater targets, a double-figure bonefish like this particularly thick-set specimen being released, is a real possibility at Islamorada. Monsters of 14-16 lbs are certainly not pipe dreams.*

Next spread *An anxious moment on board John Rawles seventeen-foot skiff for Christine Slater enjoying a spot of afternoon light-tackle sharking action over the flats, as a 100lb-plus black spinner shark breaks free whilst being unhooked. But fear not for Richard Ward (in red) or experienced charter skipper John Rawle. Wilson was the nutter wading mere feet away up to his nipples in water capturing the action with a 20mm wide-angle lens. Because when the shark angrily shot off it missed my right leg by inches. Phew!*

The hook trace is 4 feet of clear, 100lb monofilament joined to 20lb reel line on fixed spool reels, or 30lb if using multipliers. First a Bimini twist is tied at the end of the reel line and after making two half-hitches on the end of the 100lb trace, the Bimini's leading loop is threaded through. The two half-hitches are then pulled tight and to complete a four-turn uni-knot is tied around the 100lb hook trace and well lubricated with saliva before tightening and bedding down up against the half-hitches. It sounds complicated I admit, but the 'junction', which alleviates the need for a swivel and two separate knots, is easy to tie and maximizes the reel line's breaking strain – most important when contemplating battles with tarpon to 200lb on just 20lb test. The 30lb reel line on the multiplier outfits is used to drift the crab beneath a small, clip-on polystyrene float, directly downtide behind the boat, whereas the 20lb test on the fixed spool outfit allows maximum distances for casting a freelined crab either side of

Left *Hooked on a float-fished ten-inch live mullet by Pete Hazlewood, a 130lb Islamorada tarpon goes berserk as it nears the boat skippered by Lonny Shaw, following a memorable battle over shallow flats. It was Pete's second tarpon hook-up of the morning, during which our mullet were repeatedly bitten off by sizeable barracudas. Wire traces are not employed for tarpon fishing. 100lb test monofilament presents live bait more naturally whether using live blue crabs or mullet and consequently results in many more hits.*

Next spread *Pelicans wait on the post tops at Whale Harbour Marina in Islamorada for a free banquet of snapper and grunt guts, knowing full well these daily charter-boat excursions to inshore banks and reefs result in a long fish-filleting session when they return.*

the drifting skiff to feeding tarpon, and then slowly winding it in just beneath the surface until a fish grabs hold.

Now whilst it's true that a percentage of bites even during darkness are ridiculously gentle from such a monstrous fish, which somewhere between 6 and 8 feet in length and covered in huge silver scales resembles a giant herring, most feel incredibly powerful. As the hook bites home the tarpon usually responds by catapulting itself completely clear of the water's surface in a spectacular cascade of spray (sometimes repeatedly, each fish reacting entirely differently) before crashing back in again to rip anything up to 200 yards of line from your reel. They are phenomenally strong creatures. There then commences a battle that might well continue for two hours or more.

On that first morning out with John Rawle our two guests, totally mesmerized by events, both brought 100lb-plus tarpon successfully to the skiff while yours truly concentrated purely on the photography, trying to 'jump' the two he hooked as many times as possible by holding them very tight. I paid for my flippancy however by losing both – not that I really cared.

On another morning I went and hooked into a really serious-sized whopper whilst drifting some 200 yards on the Atlantic side below the Highway U.S.1 road bridge. The tarpon immediately headed uptide for the bridge with us in pursuit, badly fraying the 20lb reel line around the barnacle-encrusted bridge supports. Miraculously however the line held and within half an hour of setting the hook 200 yards below the bridge, I was now more or less the same distance above and uptide of the bridge in Florida Bay, heading for the shallow flats. The pursuit of tarpon fishing during darkness is unquestionably the most exhilarating, mind-blowing and nerve-wracking sport you are likely to experience on rod and line whilst boat fishing, believe me. You can sense the hairs standing up on the back of your neck in anticipation of a run, and it certainly brings out that primal hunting instinct in you. Half an hour later, having twice played the great fish around a marker buoy, it headed, yes you've guessed it, downtide and went straight back beneath the same road bridge again to more or less where I had first hooked it. We must have covered the best part of a mile during the hour-long fight and I was fancying my chances of getting a glimpse of the fish. Then quite suddenly the badly frayed 20lb reel line fell back limp and the rod sprang back straight. What did I say? Well I can't repeat it here, that's for sure!

To put our eight guests' tarpon safari results for the week into a nutshell would be impossible. The stories alone following each session were endless when the four skiffs carrying everyone met after fishing for breakfast at Lor-e-lei's Cabana Bar and Restaurant at around 7.30 a.m. before heading back to a few hours sleep. Though I guess the total catch of 27 tarpon landed between 65 and 160lb (most topping 100lb) with twice as many lost says it all and provided many a memorable battle to recall during cold winter evenings back home. And no doubt like myself they'll all want to come back again. Incidentally all tarpon are released, with the hope that they will live to fight another day. And when the guide finally touches the leader and gives an estimation of the fish's size it is taken as landed, whether the hook pops out as he holds the leader tight or he is able to extract the hook.

Permit sometimes take live blue crabs intended for tarpon, and John Rawle has in fact caught them close to 40lb, which is a big permit. Of course small sharks, which are all too common on the flats, also love them. For great daytime sport using chunks of cut bait, black-tip, bull, bonnethead, lemon and nurse sharks in the 10-100lb plus range or even larger, along with the occasional large barracuda, all provide great bran-tub action on a heavy freshwater spinning or light boat rod outfit, say 20lb-class gear.

The huge stingrays seen regularly patrolling across the shallow flats, monsters exceeding 200lb, are rarely fished for, due I guess to the array of more exotic species to hand. But if you have the inclination, a 50lb class boat outfit at the ready, including a strong 6/0 hook baited with fresh crab or a small whole squid and a stealthy approach, you could achieve a quick hook-up with the skiff being towed along nicely until the ray runs out of steam. Naturally your guide will assume you are completely off your trolley specifically setting out to hook a plain old stingray, when there are so many 'proper' fish about, but you'll just have to convince him otherwise. He won't agree of course, because with a fresh shrimp presented on a size 2 hook tied direct to 10-12lb mono, used in conjunction with a light to medium spinning or light carp rod outfit, you could tempt a legendary bonefish – otherwise known, due to their exceptional camouflage, as the 'shadows of the flats'. The initial scorching run of this unbelievably fast barbel-like fish can almost empty the reel. Their strength and acceleration is quite phenomenal, leaving first-time anglers staring down at their fast-emptying reel in total disbelief. What's more, double-figure bonefish are far from uncommon and a very real target around Islamorada, whereas elsewhere around the world's oceans, 8-9lb bones are rated as specimens. John Rawle has in fact taken a 15½lb bonefish on his boat using 12lb class gear, which would have become a world record. A larger fish however was taken shortly afterwards before a claim to the IGFA could be submitted.

Whether you are successful with the tarpon in Islamorada or not, a visit to Robbies in Lower Matecumbe is imperative before leaving the Keys. Here you can rent a boat, have a chilled beer or a bite to eat and actually get to feed by hand hundreds of totally wild tarpon (they are not enclosed) to over 100lb which gather in shallow water around the boat dock. For simply studying the species at close hand through crystal clear water Robbies is an absolute must, albeit somewhat frustrating to the angler who's not hooking-up.

In complete contrast to all the more usual attractions in Islamorada, during my last visit with friends Christine Slater and Simon Turner, I chartered a 32-foot exceptionally fast (40 knots) boat owned by Captain Billy Knowles, one of the most senior and most respected of all local guides, to fish a wreck over 50 miles out across the bay in the Gulf of Mexico. Unfortunately we got caught in a tropical storm after just two hours of sport and had to hightail it back in. But that's another story. Suffice to say that in a short time we sampled something different, catching jacks, cobia, a permit (nearly), plus some exceedingly large nurse sharks, would you believe to almost 300lb, on just 30lb gear and small livebaits bumped along the bottom beside the wreck in around 25 feet of water. I must try it again in better weather.

Above *Using live mullet on 30lb class gear, Norwich-based dentist and angling fanatic Simon Turner boated this powerful and magnificently marked Warsaw grouper amongst a haul of amberjacks and horse-eye jacks whilst drifting over a deepwater wreck twenty miles out into the Atlantic from Islamorada.*

Should you fancy a change with a two-hour drive down to Key West, an island that has inspired such writers as Tennessee Williams and Ernest Hemingway, you'll not be disappointed. It is actually closer to Havana (90 miles away) than to Miami, and boasts some stunning, upmarket hotels, seafood restaurants, museums, an aquarium and two- or three-day charter boat trips (you sleep on board) to the amazing deep-water reefs of the Dry Tortugas, some 70 miles out. Here you'll catch huge jewfish, mutton snappers, plus warsaw, marbled, black and tiger groupers – all guaranteed to pull your arms out of your sockets. These trips, availabe all year round, include accommodation, fresh bait and all terminal tackle, with rod-and-reel combos available for hire. Or you can take it easy

and shop around or visit Hemingway's home, now a registered national landmark where from 1931 to 1961 he penned 75 per cent of his works. There are of course party boat trips, charter boat trips and guided skiffs readily available for all the previously mentioned species from sailfish to tarpon, with fly fishing for tarpon a Key West speciality.

The sunsets seen from Key West are considered to be the most beautiful in the whole of the United States, and I'm not going to argue. Sunset celebrations occur every

Above *Simply to study this enigmatic species at close quarters and marvel in its perfect scalage, even frustrated visiting anglers who are not hooking up come to enjoy this rare spectacle at Robbies' dock in Lower*

Matecumbe, Islamorada. Here in the shallowest of crystal-clear water are hundreds of wild tarpon to close on 200lb (they are not enclosed) gathering to be fed by hand on fish scraps.

evening accompanied by the most eccentric street performers and entertainers ranging from sword swallowers and animal acts, to fire-tossing jugglers. So enjoy the sunset the Key West way. Mainstream America these Florida Keys most certainly ain't.

THE ZAMBEZI RIVER AND LAKE KARIBA
ZAMBIA/ZIMBABWE

The Zambezi River, wild, often savage, rises in north-west Zambia, continues south to the Caprivi Strip of South West Africa and then east through Zimbabwe and Mozambique to the Indian Ocean. As it meanders, it passes through some of central south Africa's most stunning countryside and game-packed national safari parks. It is the fourth longest river in Africa with an overall length of 1,700 miles. It is Africa's most easily accessible freshwater angling paradise and, together with Lake Kariba, simply has no equal. Though born and raised a Londoner, whenever I return to the warmth of the Zambezi valley in particular, I truly feel as though I am coming home again. Such is my love affair with a region steeped deeply in the history of our Victorian forefathers' attempts to 'civilize' Africa at its most raw, where cannibalism, disease, bloodshed and slavery went hand in hand with the mystique of the Zambezi River to those early explorers and missionaries.

The Zambezi is an extremely lush and incredibly fertile, ever-changing watercourse, full of tree-clad islands, vast sandbanks where pods of hippos bask, rocky rapids, awesome waterfalls cutting through deep gorges, not forgetting two major hydroelectricity schemes in Lake Kariba and Lake Cahora Bassa. Throughout its course you can experience unique game viewing whilst fishing and it is home to over 100 species of weird and wonderfully coloured and shaped freshwater fish from the giant vundu catfish, one of my all-time favourite fighters, to the colourful tooth-laden tiger fish (*Hydrocynus forskablii*), arguably the fiercest fish swimming anywhere on this planet, which is equipped with no fewer than 18 disproportionately large triangular-shaped, interlocking, razor-sharp teeth – ten in the roof of its powerful, fully-expandable mouth and eight set into the lower jaw.

The visiting angler, however, needs to accept that that ratio of tiger fish lost to those landed is six to one. They are easily the most difficult of all sportsfish, fresh or salt, to

Previous spread *Truly one of the seven natural wonders of the world, the sheer majesty of Victoria Falls (especially when viewed from above by light aircraft or helicopter), is a sight to behold. Spiritual almost. Its mile-wide escarpment, over which the Zambezi's white water roars, drops 300 feet sending great clouds of spray high into the sky. The Zambian name for these spectacular falls, named after his queen by Dr David Livingstone in 1855, is 'Mosi-oa-*

Tunya', meaning 'the Smoke that Thunders'. And it certainly does.
Above *Fancy fly-fishing for tiger fish into these wonderful rapids? This is the prolific Chobe River immediately above Ichingo Chobe River Lodge at Impalila Island, below which the Chobe and mighty Zambezi Rivers converge. Whether you choose spinners, plugs or fly, high-leaping tigers to 15lb are not uncommon here, along with barbel-type pussies and colourful predatory bream.*

keep on the hook. For despite a slamming take, which in itself would seem enough for the hook to be driven home, when the reel subsequently screams like the proverbial stuck pig, and a tiger fish comes leaping high out of the water in a cascade of spray combined with an acrobatic display of head shaking as they all do, more often than not the hook or hooks are literally catapulted out.

The furthest upriver I have so far explored is at Mezaba Bay in Zambia, a totally isolated safari lodge situated at the foot of the Barotse flood plain, just a few miles downriver from spectacular Ngonye Falls. It is not the easiest spot to reach, because a private charter to either Livingstone Airport or direct to the lodge must be arranged following an international long-haul flight to Lusaka (9 hours from Heathrow). But the A-frame thatched rooms afford breathtaking views across a rather intimate Zambezi which, averaging less than 100 yards across, is so completely different in character from the wide papyrus and reed-lined lower reaches. Here in deep swirling pools and eddies

Left *No wonder experienced international angler, Dave Priddy, looks pleased. He caught the doubles while Wilson took a string of eight-to-nine-pounders. This magnificent twelve-and-a-half-pounder literally jumped itself to a standstill after hitting an 11cm Rapala Magnum shallow diver trolled at around five knots through a wide set of rapids in the Zambezi at Murandi. Note its brilliant colours, powerful dentistry, phenomenal depth and most importantly massive weight-for-length ratio compared to Lake Nasser tiger fish. See page 15.*

Next spread *Returning to the Ichingo River Lodge at Impalila Island after an afternoon's trolling for tiger fish at Mambora Rapids on the Zambezi River. Only the words 'liquid gold' can perhaps portray the stunning beauty of this particular African sunset. Not the easiest of subjects to try and photograph from a boat zooming along at twenty knots.*

cutting through a narrow rocky gorge, which fortunately is impossible to net by the locals, live far more large crocodiles than you would associate with sets of rapids, plus tiger fish in prolific numbers, including some real beauties to 20lb and more.

The lodge boat takes you upstream into countless, mouthwatering pools where both trolling and casting from safe rocky ledges on the shore produces tigers of a high average size. The best lures are the Rapala Super Shad Raps and Magnums and a wire trace is, of course, imperative. Fly rodders will no doubt sigh in ecstasy at some of the fast runs below the Ngonye Falls. However a 10lb tiger fish connected to an English chalkstream outfit is not recommended, so we are talking reservoir or even saltwater fly rods and size 9-10 lines here, working streamer or fly patterns on strong size 6-2 hooks connected to a short wire trace and 10lb leader. Larger, longer flies simply have the end of the dressing ripped off so it's wise to persevere with smaller patterns for maximizing on hook-ups. Wherever the Zambezi widens to form deep and slow back eddies adjacent to sandbanks, the long and flat headed sharp-tooth catfish is a likely customer to bottom-fished whole small fresh dead fish or a fish fillet. These powerful fighters, also called barbel locally, reach weights in excess of 60lb, though specimens in the 10-25lb range are considered more usual catches. Incidentally, the giant vundu catfish (*Heterobronchus longifilis*), Africa's largest catfish which reaches weights over 100lb, is only found downstream of Victoria Falls.

There is a host of lesser species however to be enjoyed using ledgered or float-fished bread paste or worms and on light spinning tackle with size 1-4 Mepps-type spinners. These include silver barbel, squeekers, labeo (a carp-like fish) and several strikingly coloured species of predatory bream. The best period, particularly for tiger fish, is during September and October. Additionally, if you stay at Mezaba Bay, you can also enjoy white-water rafting or game viewing by Land Rover.

Some 70 to 80 miles downriver from Mezaba Bay, where the Chobe River merges with the Zambezi at Impalila Island, is the renowned Ichingo Chobe River Lodge, offering unique safari-style, well-aired tented accommodation (*meru*) with stunning views through jungle across the river. Impalila Island is in fact situated on the eastern tip of the Caprivi, the meeting place of four countries – Namibia, Botswana, Zimbabwe and Zambia. Game viewing by boat here in the Chobe National Park, just a short trip downstream from the lodge, affords marvellous close encounters with lion, giraffe, elephant, buffalo, hippo, antelope and many others. Visitors can also try white-water canoeing down the rapids or take the quieter approach by viewing the surrounding islands whilst being poled along by a skilful guide in a traditional dugout canoe, locally called a mekoro.

In complete contrast, with two anglers and experienced guide in each, the lodge runs four 16-foot customized fishing boats with 75hp engines to purr you along at over 30 knots to explore a variety of locations, from exciting sets of rapids in both rivers, to wild places as far as 50 miles upstream in the Zambezi. Mind-blowing pools with names like Murandi, Golden Pond, Jo Jo's and Nantunga Island, where the Zambezi varies anywhere from 100 to 300 yards across, all contain prolific concentrations of tiger fish in the 5-15lb bracket, ever eager to chomp at shallow running lures trolled at between 3 and 5 knots.

When I escorted a party of ten Brits here in September 2000, literally everyone caught hard-battling tigers over 8lb, with no fewer than nine double-figure specimens. The two most productive lures by far were Rapala Super Shad Raps and 11cm Magnum shallow divers, particularly the red-head colour pattern.

I was surprised at the generally shallow depth of the Zambezi in this area, averaging just 4-8 feet. Hot spots occur at the junctions with other rivers and drainage channels, especially around islands both at the upstream and downstream ends where shallow sandbars are created by the severe winter flooding. The larger fish definitely prefer the strongest currents over sandy gravel or a rocky bottom. Long pools were also productive as, of course, were the rapids, by far the most exciting locations of all.

At Ichingo the best tiger period is from August through until November, with September the most consistent month. There is also a potentially tiger–rich window during June and July, once high water levels start to recede at the end of the rainy season. This is when massive concentrations of juvenile shoal species work their way

Above *Following a serious morning's trolling, our party of eight lure enthusiasts from the UK take time for shore lunch and to reflect how it is that five out of every six tiger fish manage to jump themselves off the hooks. This wide, picturesque and heavily reed-lined part of the Zambezi is at Nantunga Island.*

Right *Fringing the margins along the wide, quieter reaches of the Zambezi, patches of water lilies add a splash of colour to one of Africa's most evocative locations.*

back into the main river from the wide floodplains whilst the water is still warm and heavily coloured. Tiger fish then pack into hot spots where wide channels merge with the main flow, and are caught on freelined or ledgered fish strip or freshly killed small whole fish. There are also some wonderful pools in which to fly fish for tigers in the Chobe River rapids just a short walk away from the lodge. To say that the area around Impalila Island is a twitcher's delight could even be an understatement. Some 400 species of birds have in fact been recorded here from flocks of carmine bee-eaters several hundred strong, surely one of the world's most breathtakingly beautiful birds, to the extremely rare African flightless fin foot.

Along the river's course, hippo, elephant, waterbuck, huge monitor lizards and enormous crocodiles were our daily fishing companions as were giant pied and even the tiny, brilliantly coloured malachite kingfishers. Add night herons, egrets and open-billed storks, with fish eagles and yellow-billed kites for ever casting a watchful eye at our shallow running, trolled lures from high above and you have all the ingredients of a truly evocative environment. There is, of course, always a downside, and in Africa death, undoubtedly more evident than elsewhere, is usually portrayed by hundreds of vultures working the thermals high overhead. One afternoon whilst trolling for tiger fish close to the Mambora rapids, an awful stench suddenly filled our nostrils, the result of Zambian ivory poachers who had crossed the river and shot three elephants on a reed-covered island. What an upsetting sight for the sake of a few ivory tusks. The carcasses were almost picked dry and covered in the largest maggots I've even seen, whilst perched in the tall trees close by were several hundred vultures and marabou storks, their bellies bloated full.

Whenever we fancied a diversion from trolling for tiger fish we changed over from fast-tip rods, 30lb braided reel lines and multiplier reels to light telescopic spinning outfits and 10lb monofilament reel lines, to work size 4-5 Mepps-type spinners between the gaps in the marginal covering of tall reeds and papyrus. For extra fun I employed my 5-foot American baitcasting stick and baby multiplier combo. Our

quarry was any one of no fewer than eight colourful species of predatory bream within the 2-6lb size range. With names like pink happies, thin face, large mouth, humpback and robustus, all are members of the mouthbrooding tilapia family. The robustus also called nembwe locally and robbies throughout the Zambezi system, averaged 3-4lb apiece and were resplendent in their striking livery of olive green, yellow and blue. They provided marvellous, arm-wrenching action in shallow marginal runs beneath choice habitats of weed rafts and inlets or gaps between clumps of papyrus.

Some were caught with the boat stemming the current or working slowly upriver. Or the boat's bows were pointed into the dense marginal cover enabling casts to be made parallel to the shoreline. In really slow currents back drifting downstream just 10 yards out from the shore permitted casts to be made right into the choicest lies

Above *Using a beaten-up orange Rapala he'd found, trolled on a thick hand line behind his dugout canoe whilst rowing along the Zambezi at Golden Pond, this fourteen-year-old local lad demonstrated how it should be done by landing a huge tiger fish of over 20lb. Makes you wonder what we were doing with thousands of pounds of designer hi-tech reels, rods, lines and lures in our possession doesn't it? Makes you want to cry!*

Can there be any more colourful adversary for the taking on a lightweight baitcasting outfit than this robustus predatory bream? These hard-battling members of the tilapia family are to be found anywhere along the upper Zambezi where tall reeds and papyrus beds fringe the margins to provide overhead cover.

amongst the marginal entanglement thus covering maximum territory – my favourite technique incidentally. It was imperative to get the spinner quickly down 3-4 feet to the riverbed and start a slow retrieve immediately. These aggressive bream often locked on to the spinner as its blade flapped down to the bottom, and grabbed hold on the first or second turn of the reel handle. Another method used in really fast-flowing sections of the river was to slowly troll a small deep diving plug really close beside the marginal cover, thus encouraging bream to venture out and attack. And whichever method was employed there were always exotic surprises in store in the form of a double-figure sharp-toothed catfish or modest-sized tiger fish, both of which put up quite spectacular battles on light tackle.

Some ten miles downstream of Impalila Island is another wonderful lodge specializing in game viewing and fishing at Imbabala Safari Camp, which is landscaped into beautiful riverine forest just an hour's drive upriver from Victoria Falls. The thatched chalets in this most scenic setting all enjoy a truly panoramic view over the Zambezi which opposite the camp is wide and slow. There breathtakingly colourful water lilies fringe the dense marginal growth. I caught numerous tiger fish to over 14lb here whilst trolling above the huge set of rapids situated downriver from the camp during the early 1990s when filming for television. The sight one evening of over 300 elephants coming down to bathe and drink from the river as the sun set while we sipped cool sundowners from the camp's viewing pontoon, will remain in my memory forever. Zimbabwe's national parks do in fact boast the largest herds of elephants in Africa.

Memories of rock hopping along the rapids using both fly and spinning tackle to catch predatory bream, labeo and tiger fish are pretty strong too. A trick I learnt from the guide here, which has subsequently worked for me with predators all over the world, was to bait the spinner's treble hook with a bunch of redworms. They certainly made everything I caught hang on that much longer. Another ruse, designed to make tiger fish hold on longer when trolling, was replacing the treble of a Mepps Aglia Longue with a size 3/0 or 4/0 single, and adding a bunch of worms, or better still a narrow strip of fresh flesh cut from the white belly of a tiger fish. The large single certainly appears to find better purchase behind those wicked teeth. Incidentally, whilst small tigers can be lifted out, specimens should be netted and great care taken in removing the hook. One jump or shake of those awesome jaws could all too easily remove a finger or at least inflict a nasty wound. I hold them tight by inserting my left forefinger and middle finger into the tiger's left gill opening and then clamp down firmly on the outside with my thumb – similar to the grip I use for pike and zander. After unhooking, the fish is then in a perfect grip to raise up either vertically or horizontally (your right hand supporting its belly) for an impressive trophy picture prior to release.

Except where interrupted by occasional rapids the Zambezi continues placid and smooth flowing, with sport for all the previously mentioned species continuing all the way downstream to magnificent Victoria Falls, truly one of the seven natural wonders of the world. Named after Queen Victoria by explorer Dr David Livingstone

in 1855, these falls are the largest and arguably the most beautiful on our planet. The falls, which consist of a curtain of thundering white water over a mile wide and 300 feet high, plunging into a churning maelstrom below, sending great clouds of spray several hundred feet high into the sky, may be viewed from numerous points along the opposite side of the chasm. Alternatively they can be viewed from the air either by helicopter or light aircraft, known as the Flight of Angels, during half-hourly excursions – a breathtaking, some would even call it a hairy experience, if ever there was one. The Zambian people have a special name for these spectacular falls, Mosi-oa-Tunya meaning 'the Smoke that Thunders' – and it truly does.

Attractions at Victoria Falls include evening upriver booze cruises on the Zambezi; tribal dancing either in the craft village or in the Victoria Falls Hotel itself, said to be amongst the world's top ten; a crocodile ranch; or a walk across the bridge spanning the Zambezi gorge between Zimbabwe and Zambia. Here you get the most incredible view both up and downstream with a drop of over 300 feet down to the rocky river rapids below and believe it or not it is a spot from where you can book the world's highest bungee jump. White-water rafting down the thunderous rapids of the gorge is yet another option to be enjoyed by visitors.

Upon leaving Victoria Falls the Zambezi continues in an easterly direction through the narrow, steadily deepening Batoka Gorge and into the broad Guembe Valley for a distance of over 80 miles to the picturesque shores of Lake Kariba, which at 175 miles long and in places up to 30 miles wide, is one of the largest man-made lakes on this planet. Just imagine a sheet of still water stretching from London to Exeter and you have Kariba which covers over 3,000 square miles of former forests and savannah, roughly the same landmass as Wales. In Bantu the word kariba implies menace, and relates to a huge rock (now hidden below the surface and never to be seen again) situated at the entrance of Kariba Gorge, which was once considered to be the home of the river god, Nyaminyani, whose power could cause both humans and canoes alike to be sucked down into the bowels of this former awesome river gorge to their certain destruction. Moreover what the Zambezi's rocks could not accomplish was surely finished off by the huge crocodiles living in the gorge. The book *Kariba – The Struggle with the River God* written by Frank Clements in 1959 (highly recommended) on the completion of the dam (which provides hydroelectric power for vast areas of central south Africa), makes fascinating reading. It describes the creation of the 420-foot-high and 80-foot-thick wall, which spans 1,900 feet across the gorge, carrying a 40-foot-wide road linking Zimbabwe to Zambia. The author also relates how African tribes (29,000 people in all) were relocated, albeit against their will, from what is now the lake bed, to areas higher up the valley, and Operation Noah in which thousands of wild animals of the Zambezi valley were rescued by boat from drowning and certain starvation as the lake started to fill. The most fascinating tale of all relates how twice during successive years in 1957 and 1958, as a result of horrific flooding, the worst ever in the history of the valley, the river god came close to destroying the combined efforts and civil engineering skills of highly specialized teams from England, France and Italy. But despite Nyaminyani, the Kariba Dam was completed and has since

Above *Completed in 1959 with an eighty-foot thick wall of concrete stretching 1,900 feet from bank to bank across the Zambezi River at the Kariba Gorge, this massive dam created Lake Kariba, which at over 170 miles long is still one of the largest man-made lakes on the planet. Its turbines provide hydro-electric power for vast areas of both Zambia and Zimbabwe.*

afforded the travelling angler with unparalleled sportsfishing – whilst game viewing. The most direct route to Kariba is a nine-hour long-haul flight from Heathrow to Zimbabwe's capital, Harare followed by a short domestic flight direct to Kariba Airport. Marineland is then just 20 minutes away by road.

As large proportions of both the Zambian and Zimbabwean shorelines are taken up with safari and national parks, anglers are obliged to boat fish, because it is an offence, and downright dangerous anyway, to venture ashore. The wild animals have become used to this fact and so tolerate the presence of anglers' boats at astonishingly close range. Herds of buffalo and several antelope species, plus elephants, are literally daily sightings along the shoreline whilst fishing or moving from one area to another, as are pods of hippos and massive crocodiles. Troops of chattering baboons also appear

to be everywhere and it is not unusual to see a pride of lions shading themselves during the heat of the day beneath tall trees literally within yards of the lake's edge.

It is well worth investing in the very best pair of binoculars (my ideal being 10x42) you can afford before going afloat on this totally unique environment. For, in addition to animals of the savannah, the bird life on Kariba is quite phenomenal. For fishing trips day boats with a guide can be hired from Marineland harbour at Kariba, or better still spend a week or more exploring the lake on board a cruiser. Locally these craft are simply called houseboats because you live and sleep on board, but each day you fish from one of the 12-14-foot customized angling tenders it tows. Cruisers come in a variety of sizes from 30 to over 60 feet in length accommodating entire families or parties of up to ten anglers. Some have three decks and are even fitted with air-conditioned rooms – 120 degrees Fahrenheit is not unheard of on the lake. Personally however, so I can really enjoy the evocative nature of Africa, I much prefer to sleep up on deck at night. That marvellous mixture of African spices, hot sultry air and the sound of a thousand frogs riveting away, followed as dawn breaks by the blood-curdling bellow of a bull hippo or the haunting cry of a fish eagle, combine to make fishing on Kariba an outstanding experience.

For almost a decade whilst filming, holidaying and when escorting groups of anglers to Kariba on behalf of Tailor Made Holidays, I have stayed on board a wonderful 55-foot long cruiser called *Mirimba*. It comes complete with four fishing tenders, a

Above *Because large areas of both the Zambian and Zimbabwean shorelines around Lake Kariba are taken up with safari and national parks, visitors can enjoy unrivalled game viewing whilst fishing. It is in fact illegal to venture ashore and this is something which the wild animals are very much aware, so close-quarter viewing of elephant, giraffe, buffalo, baboons, hippos, various antelopes, wading birds, crocodiles and even lions, is the norm rather than the exception.*

Above *Henry is a decidedly friendly hippo, unlike most in the Zambezi River, which can become extremely dangerous when approached at close quarters. He is a firm favourite with guests at the Royal Zambezi Lodge on the Zambian side of these wide reaches adjacent to the Lower Zambezi National Park, spending most of the day asleep on a nearby sandbank.*

crewman, a fabulous cook called Timothy, and King, the skipper, who knows the lake like the back of his hand. King always ensures there is enough fishing bait on board in the way of a box full of earthworms, plus numerous packets of frozen kapenta, a 2-4-inch long freshwater sardine which is the staple food of many predatory species in the lake, particularly tiger fish. Kapenta were stocked into Kariba in 1962 from Lake Tanganyika where they grow considerably larger (up to 6 inches in length) because the water is warmer, and became so well established after five years they have been commercially harvested since 1968. King also arranges for several large bars of blue soap to be on board. Yes, blue soap, which is by far the most selective bait for catching the legendary vundu catfish, although the occasional large sharp-tooth catfish will take it to. I think they are attracted to the particular animal oils that ooze into the water from which this cheap blue soap is manufactured. Bunches of kapenta, any small freshly killed fish, a huge bunch of worms or half an ox heart (a favourite local offering) will also catch vundu but they each also attract every other toothy, blood-lusting weird and wonderful species inhabiting the lake from tiger fish to snapping turtles. Another bait I have found successful is any rubbery brand of luncheon meat. I carefully thread about half a tin on to a size 6/0 with the aid of a baiting needle. I am certain that a large ball of trout or carp pellet paste would also do the business. My brother Dave has been successful with vundu when prebaiting an area (around his cruiser tied up beside a deep channel) for several days with large, oily salmon pellets, although he relied

upon soap for hook baits. The very best way of presenting it is to knead well into a chicken egg-sized lump and hide a size 6/0 hook inside. My preference however is for the Drennan, stainless steel O'Shaunessey pattern which has never shown the slightest sign of opening or distorting during over ten years of landing both mahseer and vundu to close on 100lb. My line choice, in conjunction with an ABU 10000 multiplier, for both species incidentally, is 35lb test monofilament. For vundu I add a strong swivel, then a 4-foot hook trace of 45-50lb monofilament which withstands the abrasive pads of tiny teeth situated in both the upper and lower jaws.

Now whilst vundu are spread all over the lake and can be expected from just about anywhere, they are particularly attracted to deep river gorges and areas around river mouths and drainage entrances, even shallow bays where pods of hippos colour the water, allowing attack more by feel than by sight. Vundu are equipped with particularly small, piggy eyes, and like many species of cats when either of their two long sensory whiskers or barbules, which are angled to the front in feeding or scavenging mode, touch a potential meal, one vacuum-like gulp from that cavernous mouth and the prey is history.

My favourite vundu area on Kariba is in the steep-sided Sanyati Gorge which enters via the southern corner. At a spot called Second Crossroads the water varies between 10 and 30 feet deep and is over 100 yards wide. But more importantly, the bottom is completely free of snags and the water is usually far more coloured than out in the lake proper. This permits drift fishing (with the boat side on to the wind) slowly through the centre channel using soap or luncheon meat, bouncing the bait slowly along the bottom, 30-50 yards behind the boat. If the wind picks up, as it can especially during the later afternoon, a fly fishing drogue is used to slow the boat's drift. And when a vundu picks up the bait (I prefer to have the reel in free spool with my thumb on the line) a blistering run usually materializes. I then slam the multiplier into gear once a few yards have evaporated, point the rod at the fish until the line is humming tight before whacking the rod back hard to pull the hook through the bait into the fish. There then follows what size for size is arguably the fastest, most powerful battle (save for a mahseer) from these wide headed, awesome cats you are ever likely to experience with a heavyweight freshwater predator anywhere on this planet. And as vundu are common in the 30-70lb bracket, you can look forward to a scrap lasting anything up to half an hour or more. Though vundu are occasionally caught over 100lb, the largest I have actually encountered is a 95lb beauty, which I hooked but chose to share the fight with a guest, Ruth Taylor from Huntingdon, who had only ever caught a mackerel before.

Over the years I have experienced some incredibly hectic sport with vundu during three- and four-day stints in the Sanyati Gorge before exploring other locations around the lake. One morning in particular stands out in my memory because it epitomizes the magic of Kariba's unique combined angling and game viewing experience. I was awaiting a vundu run at the time but my attention was taken away from the rod tip to halfway up the steep-sided hill to my right thickly covered in thorn scrub, mahogany, mopani, tamarind trees and tall grasses where a small group of bush buck suddenly took fright, the darker-coloured ram honking loudly in fear. The penetrating sound cut the still morning air like a knife and I was soon to understand why they had shot through the seemingly impenetrable dry jungle of the gorge like bats out of hell. A magnificent leopard suddenly came into view over a rocky outcrop hunched down on its powerful front limbs ready to pounce. But the bush bucks were long gone. Only a family of hornbills in the trees above remained. Then, the metallic screech of the multiplier's ratchet brought me back to reality with a thud (I had flicked the ratchet on when picking up the binoculars) and I was fast into a hefty vundu. What magic.

Fishing off the back of the cruiser when it is tied up to trees on the shore, whether in the Sanyati Gorge or elsewhere on the lake, provides great fun fishing using an Avon or light carp rod outfit coupled to 10lb monofilament. Several handfuls of kapenta

Above *Amid the tall, parched hills of the Sanyati Gorge, Mirimba's skipper, 'King', prepares to slip the capacious landing net beneath a near-70lb vundu catfish. It provided UK angler Paul Phelan with an unforgettable forty-five-minute battle. The successful bait? A chicken-egg-sized lump of blue soap – honestly!*

are scattered around the fishing area, and you follow in with say a couple of kapenta on a size 6-2 hook with a swan shot pinched on to the line to take the bait down to the bottom. You could then be in for catching a dozen or more different exotic species from squeeker catfish, electric catfish, sharp-tooth catfish or even a vundu, to silver barbel, nkupe, eels, chessa, Cornish jacks (a long, strange-looking species with a tapered snout), bream and tiger fish. If you want to catch bream – and there are several species including the colourful, predatory types already mentioned (by far the most popular eating fish with the locals incidentally) – float fishing worms on light float tackle (a waggler rig is ideal) close beside and into holes amongst the dense beds of marginal weed, is by far the most effective technique. And they are great fun. If you choose to catch tiger fish, a 12-14-inch wire trace of 25-30lb braided wire and size 1 or 1/0 hook is imperative, and I up my reel line to 15lb test. Though quality tigers are taken from the Sanyati, the best opportunity of doing battle with this unique, acrobatic predator is by fishing 'in the sticks' out on the lake proper. The 'sticks' simply refers to the tops of millions of petrified tree tops, now bleached white by the sun, seen all around the irregularly contoured shoreline and around mid-lake islands, which were former hardwood forests prior to the creation of the Kariba Dam and the flooding of the Zambezi valley.

Due to the wealth of small shoal fishes inhabiting 'the sticks' tiger fish are always close by, so tying the tender up to the top of a tree usually guarantees some action. It's a strange phenomenon. A couple of handfuls of kapenta scattered around the boat will soon attract tigers if in the area and the ensuing battles to a freelined bunch of kapenta (add a swan shot for casting if necessary) are spectacular to say the least. It has to be said that more tiger fish are lost through shaking the hook out during their acrobatic leaps, or wrapping the line around sunken branches, than are ever landed – but that's the mystique of it all. Other species obviously come into the frame whilst seeking tigers amongst 'the sticks'. Squeeker catfish, sharp-tooth cats and even the occasional vundu are liable to gobble up bunches of kapenta that remain on the bottom for too long, though trying to extract a sizeable vundu hooked on tiger tackle from these sunken forests is, in my experience, a virtual impossibility. Nevertheless I have always had fun trying by untying the tender and following the vundu's route until it becomes totally unextricable.

Other difficult to land adversaries include snapping turtles, the size of dustbin lids, and crocodiles. Yes, crocs! One evening, following yet another of Kariba's magnificent sunsets, I watched a guest fishing from the stern of *Mirimba* hook into what was obviously a large croc, and which, judging by the angle of his line illuminated in the lights from the top deck (though he seemed totally oblivious to the fact) had actually climbed out on to the shore. Needless to say discretion being the better part of valour, a break-off was both desirable and inevitable.

For those perhaps more interested in bird spotting or game viewing with the occasional fishing trip thrown in, I can recommend the lake's two premier islands situated in the southern sector: Fothergill and Spurwing. Both enjoy spectacular views across Kariba to the Matusadonna mountains and game reserve, and share a distinct African bush feel. Both also offer game viewing by Land Rover, boat or canoe, plus quick access by speedboat to the Sanyati Gorge.

I cannot possibly depart from Kariba without mentioning one of the world's greatest freshwater game fishing competitions, held here every October. This is the famous International Tiger Tournament (now in its fortieth year) which attracts over 1,000 competitors from all over the globe split up into 300 or more teams fishing in boats, ranging from outboard-powered dinghies to state-of-the-art cruisers. The event, said to be the largest of its type in the world (a tented village is erected at Charara specifically for competitors) spans three days, with a 6 a.m. start each day from Charara Point, and produces an amazing number of specimen-sized tiger fish to over 20lb at the weigh-in each evening. Kariba tiger fish, decidedly deeper in the body than river fish, have in fact been taken to over 30lb, which is nothing compared to the goliath tiger fish (*Hydrocurus goliath*) of the Congo River in the Democratic Republic of the Congo (formerly Zaire) which reaches weights in excess of 100lb. I thoroughly recommend the book *The Largest Tiger Fish in the World – 'The Goliath'*, written by Belgian sportsfisherman, Douglas Dann. You will never wish to swim in tropical freshwater ever again after reading it.

Incidentally, also worth seeing before leaving Lake Kariba is the crocodile farm which exhibits monsters getting on for 20 feet long. And should you fancy exploring further down the lake from Kariba, I would suggest the picturesque Bumi River which enters from the Zimbabwean shoreline. The fishing here can be really excellent and there is a magnificent lodge at Tiger Bay where in the heat of the day you can swim in the pool or sip chilled beer.

Downstream from Kariba Gorge the Lower Zambezi continues in a huge north-easterly curve towards the Indian Ocean, now an incredibly wide river, having been joined by the Kafue River just south of Lusaka, the capital of Zambia. Famous Mana Pools National Park covers a huge chunk of the southern Zimbabwean shoreline, whilst the Chongue River enters from the Zambian side. Situated here is the renowned Royal Zambezi Lodge, just ten minutes from the Lower Zambezi National Park, justly famous for its game viewing and prolific action with huge tiger fish (doubles are common here) and vundu to test the tackle of the most discerning angler. The area is also a veritable bird watchers' paradise.

The Zambezi then enters the gorge of Cahora Bassa where, once again, the might of the river has been harnessed to create hydroelectricity with a dam wall over 500 feet high. Lake Cahora Bassa is in fact over 100 feet deeper than Kariba, and although

Left *Even the ladies catch big 'uns from the wild and fertile reaches of the lower Zambezi, downstream from the Kariba Dam. With elephants looking on, tour operator Christine Slater (right) helps display a near-14lb tiger fish caught on free-lined fish strip by my wife Jo, following an arm-wrenching, tail-walking tussle. Just look at those wicked teeth. On the fish, of course.*

Above *Italian sportsfishing journalist Roberto Ferrario enjoys the acrobatic antics of a kariba tiger fish, hooked in a quiet, shallow bay. Again freelined kapenta was the successful bait.*

roughly the same length (180 miles) is only half Kariba's volume. It nevertheless houses a far more powerful generating station and will no doubt one day also provide outstanding sportsfishing. For the present there is little adjacent infrastructure with access only through the Zimbabwean border. The Zambezi then bisects Mozambique, finally entering the Indian Ocean north of Beira via an enormous delta. Its life is now ended, but didn't it have a great time along the way.

RIO EBRO & RIO SEGRE
SPAIN

Most holidaymakers adore Spain for its sandy beaches, bustling cities and resorts active in night life. Anglers in the know, however, rate its largest watershed, the River Ebro – which rises in the Pyrenees and meanders in an easterly direction for over 700 miles through stunning scenery before entering the Mediterranean south of Barcelona through an immense delta in the region of Catalonia – the most prolific, accessible and exciting catfishing in the whole of Europe. This is a mammoth claim to make but in my opinion is absolutely just. This phenomenon has, incredibly, taken only 30 years to evolve, such is the breeding and growing capacity of the Wels catfish (first introduced into the river during the 1970s by German anglers), with subsequent stockings of bleak, zander and black bass to complement the food source and sportsfish stocks. Indigenous species of the Rio Ebro system include barbel, carp, roach, rudd, pike and eels, plus crayfish and terrapins.

I first sampled the Ebro back in the late 1980s, long before this extraordinary explosion of zander and catfish throughout the entire system, whilst researching and filming for television along the last 50 miles of the lower reaches between the picturesque weir at Tivenys and Jesus i Maria in the delta. I then rated the river the most carp-packed I had ever experienced, comparable perhaps only to Canada's Red River in Winnipeg. Now, however, it has quite literally become Europe's most prolific fish factory. I couldn't help but arrive at this conclusion following a week's marvellous sport on the river in March 2001 with old friends Keith Lambert and Simon Clarke of the Catfish Conservation Group, who for two decades have pioneered the pursuit of Wels catfish all over Europe. Our destination was the town of Mequinenza situated at the wide junction of the River Ebro and River Segre, some 30 miles south of Lleida, just a two-hour drive from Barcelona Airport, following a two-hour flight from the UK.

Previous spread In a stunning mountainous setting overlooking the Spanish town of Mequinenza, where the coloured waters of the River Segre (left) converge with the noticeably clearer River Ebro, live one of the most prolific concentrations of jumbo-sized wels catfish in the whole of Europe. Just a two-hour flight from British airports.

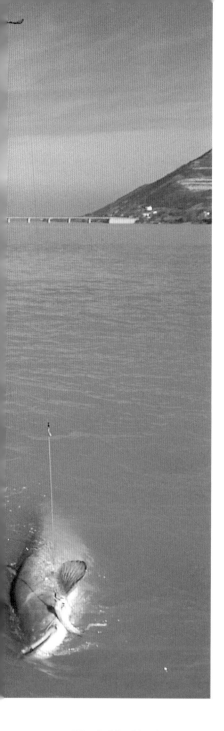

Above *Watched by Mequinenza guide Gary Allen, Keith Lambert editor of the Catfish Conservation Group's UK colour magazine* Whiskers, *gently eases to the boat an 85lb wels catfish. Hooked in over twenty feet of heavily coloured water at the wide confluence of the Rivers Segre and Ebro on an American rubber 'Bull Dawg' jerk bait, this pussy proved that despite minimal visibility artificial lures do tempt catfish.*

Here amongst spectacular scenery where kites, ospreys, vultures and storks overlook ancient castles on the hilltops, with the entire valleys of both rivers bathed in pink from the blossom of almond and peach trees, live some of the most monstrous catfish in Europe. They share this haven with an unbelievable head of common carp ranging from a seemingly endless supply of 1-5 pounders to deep-bodied, fully scaled beauties of over 40lb. Small wonder that Wels catfish grow so rapidly here and more importantly, so huge. I photographed a pair of leviathans on consecutive mornings for instance caught by German and Austrian anglers weighing a staggering 181lb and 185lb respectively. The first was caught on a 7-inch rubber shad, and must rate as one of the largest catfish ever taken on an artificial lure.

Fishing here is all made possible by the Bavarian Guiding Service which operates boats and provides tackle, excellent guides and accommodation for visiting anglers at its purpose-built camp situated just 30 yards from the banks of the River Segre in Mequinenza. This excellent self-catering camp, which is open all year, can accommodate up to 70 anglers. During our stay catfishers from France, Germany, Switzerland, Belgium, Holland, Luxembourg and the UK provided a distinct international camaraderie with some interesting conversations around the weekly barbecue.

In addition to producing Wels catfish of world-record class, from the surrounding area within a mile either way of the Segre's junction with the Ebro, guests account for over 1,000 catfish annually, with every fourth (on average) fish topping the 100lb mark. And every so often an unusual and highly prized albino cat is caught, the largest on record here weighing 146lb. Incidentally the best catfishing months here are March and April and again after their spawning cycle (during May and June) throughout September and October. The hottest months are July and August when temperatures soar to over 86 degrees Fahrenheit, although it doesn't stop the catfish from feeding. The coldest time of the year is during January and February when daytime temperatures drop to 42 to 44 degrees Fahrenheit.

The source of the Segre is near Sierra Del Cadi close to the French border, and it is joined by the Rio Cinca and the Rio Noguera Ribagor Cana, before converging with the Ebro at Mequinenza. It varies between just 3 and 15 feet deep, between 100 and 400 yards across and is invariably well coloured. There is always the possibility of levels in either river fluctuating enormously overnight due to either heavy rainfall far upstream in the mountains, or release of water from the hydroelectric dams constructed across the Ebro. The largest of these is situated immediately upstream of the road bridge at Mequinenza and has created depths of 50 feet plus throughout the centre of the river which is now virtually a lake for over 20 miles upstream to the town of Caspe.

There are several interesting and unusual methods used to catch these big catfish, the most effective by far being buoy fishing, a technique I had not previously used, the best bait being a carp in the 1-2lb range which are easily caught quivertipping along the margins using a single grain of sweetcorn on a size 10 hook, in conjunction with an open-end (ground bait-packed) feeder. The livebait is then mounted on a 3-foot trace of 200lb test Kevlar (to withstand the catfish's abrasive gripping pads, which consist

of thousands of tiny teeth, inside its jaws) and comprises a single 6/0 plus two 4/0 trebles with a 2oz barrel lead above the swivel. The rods are powerful fibreglass 10 footers (to keep the line above the surface) sporting multipliers loaded with 120lb braid. Buoy fishing revolves around suspending each bait beneath a large polystyrene float (the old Gazette type) a few feet above bottom, with a 10-foot 'break line' of 15lb mono connecting a snap swivel on the reel line above the float to an anchored buoy. This permits baits to be positioned accurately over choice areas without fear of them roaming all over the river and tangling other lines.

The most important person involved in this mode of fishing is your guide and we were in the most experienced hands of Gary Allen from St. Albans in Hertfordshire, who has been guiding at Mequinenza for three years. As Gary dropped each buoy on its own anchor line into position, sometimes as far as 150 yards out, he then connected the break line, dropped the livebait over the side of the boat and whilst thumbing the multiplier to release line, motored back to the bank. Each rod was then positioned upright in its own rest and the line wound down tight. It was then a waiting game from our mid-afternoon start (we were bait catching during the mornings) to when the catfish started switching hard on the feed either as dusk fell or a couple of hours into darkness. All-night fishing is illegal in Spain and on most evenings we had packed up by 10 or 11 p.m., having experienced somewhere between two and eight hits, most of which snapped the break line (hence its name) causing the rod to violently spring back and indicate a bite. Sometimes, however, the rod simply lurched full over and carried on bending. Either way the cat was struck instantly.

We took it in turns on the rods so whoever hooked-up clambered swiftly into the boat (winding like crazy to keep up with the catfish) which was then skilfully steered away from or between the other lines by Gary throughout the ensuing battle. And didn't those cats pull – we had unbelievable gut-busting fights on what I considered to be heavy tackle. On the following morning however, due to river levels dropping drastically overnight, I appreciated why we needed such gear and why we had to be quick to get above a hooked catfish in the boat. Indeed it would have been virtually impossible to land fish from the bank as the entire bay was littered with the protruding tree stumps of former forests, cleared before the lower Segre became permanently flooded. But that's all part of the crazy world of hooking into these huge catfish and on our first night, after missing two runs, we accounted for two babies of 25lb apiece, one of 89lb and a beauty of 126lb to Keith. The second night was even better, producing another four cats including a 136lb monster for Simon and a 116lb fish for me, which was by far my largest catfish ever.

Having enjoyed success so quickly by buoy fishing we decided to diversify by working large synthetic lures (Bull Dawg jerkbaits) close to the bottom in 20 feet of water at the junction of the Segre and Ebro. Keith struck gold within just half an hour with a fat 85lb fish, but that was our only hit in three sessions. However, I am sure this technique would really produce in higher water temperatures when the cats become far more aggressive. The river incidentally was running at between just 50 and 52 degrees Fahrenheit during our stay.

From the same area of the junction but in the noticeably clearer water of the Ebro, we experienced fantastic action with zander into double figures. My favourite method here was to mount a fresh bleak (caught on maggots from around the camp's floating boat dock) on a Drachkovitch rig, which incorporates two trebles and a lead ballweight, and work it up and down (in a sink-and-draw motion) close to the rocky bottom. Rubber shads mounted in the same way also produced. We enjoyed more zander action when Gary trailed his boat 20 miles upriver to the town of Caspe. Here the dammed River Ebro varies between 40 and 800 yards across and up to 50 feet through the centre channel with lots of interesting drop-offs. The zander however were in the shallow bays

and after a couple of hours of fun, using small shads on Drachko rigs it was time to catch catfish by 'klonking'.

What's klonking? Well it is a totally bizarre way of attracting Wels catfish up to the boat by playing on their inherent curiosity. You lower down a livebait, which in our case were 12-14-inch eels hooked once only through the middle with a 7/0 connected to a 3-foot trace of 200lb Kevlar, with a large barrel lead fixed just above the swivel. (The eels we brought from the camp, incidentally, where they are readily available to guests.) The klonker itself is a wooden (or stainless steel) hand device about the size of a bicycle pump with a bulbous end. This you smash firmly down on the surface of the water at regular intervals, creating a strange klonking sound from bursting air bubbles. Then, believe it or not (I am totally converted), catfish start appearing on the sonar screen whether you are at anchor or on the drift, sometimes within mere minutes of starting to klonk. On Gary's Lowrance x 75 screen we could even pinpoint at which depth both our baits and the catfish were working and subsequently lower or raise our livebaits accordingly. It was rather like playing a computer game only with real fish and utterly, utterly fascinating. Due to low water temperatures the cats were not aggressively interested in our baits, and we managed to induce just five hits, unfortunately missing four of these on the strike. I got lucky on the fifth and last hit, however, and duly landed a 70lb cat. I honestly cannot wait to try the technique of klonking again. Maybe I'll try it out on African catfish such as the vundu inhabiting the Zambezi River and Lake Kariba, or on Lake Nasser where catfish are particularly difficult to locate.

On our last afternoon/evening session Gary took us several miles up the Segre to a fast, winding stretch averaging just 50 yards across (not unlike the middle reaches of the Wye) with turbulent pools, smooth glides, huge eddies and heavily tree-lined banks. To me it certainly looked more like a barbel and salmon river, but once darkness loomed over the valley, those cats came out to play and started worrying our baits, buoy fished in a huge slack along the opposite bank. Simon landed an 80 pounder, Keith a beauty of 118lb, which went berserk once it got into the main flow, and I pulled the hooks from what felt like a modest-sized fish. It was a great end to a fabulous week's action. And for anyone wishing to realize the dream of catching a freshwater fish in excess of that magical 100lb target, not too far from home, I can think of nowhere to compete with those Mequinenza whoppers.

WATAMU
KENYA

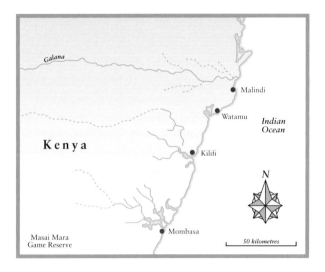

Bordered by Tanzania, Uganda, the Sudan, Ethiopia, Somalia and the Indian Ocean with additional shoreline around Lake Victoria and Lake Turkana – two of Africa's greatest lakes – plus a mountainous region and more than a dozen massive game parks, Kenya is indeed a country truly blessed. Whether you fly in on a direct flight from London to its capital Nairobi, or from other African cities, the distinct greenness of Kenya's rich farmlands is quite unmistakable. Its offshore blue-water sportsfishing is arguably amongst the most prolific in the whole world.

Previous spread *Amidst a beautiful tranquil morning at Watamu bay, tenders packed with big-game anglers are transported to their respective craft, to do battle with some of Kenya's most powerful and thrilling adversaries, giant kingfish and wahoo, the colourful dorado, yellow-fin tuna, giant trevally or gladiators such as sail fish, broad-bill swordfish and marlin.*

Left *Blue-water sportsfishing enthusiast and angling tour operator Buck Hunt, of Hunt Travel, sifts through a veritable armoury of colourful kona-head marlin lures on the way out to the trolling grounds.*

For instance what can possibly be nicer than sipping a chilled beer in equatorial Africa in a bar full of tackle and photographic memorabilia of the great Ernest Hemingway, with wonderfully preserved examples of the sea's most charismatic species like marlin, broad-bill swordfish, huge sharks and warsaw groupers lining the walls, whilst admiring stunning views overlooking the tropical blue water of the Indian Ocean? You can experience this at Hemingways Resort, situated at Watamu on the Kenyan–East African coastline 20 miles south of Malindi and 70 miles north of Mombasa, with flights from both airports direct to Nairobi. The three-storey, thatched accommodation, with all rooms overlooking a mass of colourful shrubs and two swimming pools, providing spectacular panoramic views through tall coconut palms to the ocean, is a veritable haven to blue-water enthusiasts. Hemingways specializes in big game fishing for marlin, broad-bill swordfish and sailfish, with an exciting list of arm-wrenching battlers such as yellow-fin tuna, barracuda, wahoo, dorado, kingfish, cobia, and several species of jacks also likely to grab your trolled kona-head lures, Rapala Magnums, frigate mackerel or small bonito livebaits, mounted fish-strip baits or simple squid skirt-jigs.

The secret with offshore trolling is to follow the flocks of birds (mostly terns) feeding on sardines or mantis prawns pushed up to the surface by frigate mackerel, bonito, jacks or yellow-fin tuna. Lures and baits are then trolled around the mêlée in a wide circle. And as kingfish, wahoo, barracudas or billfish could be lying beneath, quite literally anything may be raised and subsequently hooked from a 10lb jack to a quarter-ton marlin. It's exotic, bran-tub fishing at its most spectacular as my wife Jo and I experienced in February 2001 during a week's stay at Hemingways in the company of our good friends Stewart and Ellen Smalley from Aldeburgh in Suffolk. Being an east-coast skipper himself (operating out of Orford) and specializing in bass, Stewart organized a two-man trolling boat so we guys could explore alternate mornings between organized all-day charter trips on board the 35-foot boats when our wives came along. Incidentally, our stay coincided with a huge bloom of mantis prawn, stretching from Shimoni in the south all the way north to Kiwayn, a distance of over 200 miles. Such concentrations of this crustacean had not been seen since the 1970s.

It was most enjoyable capturing the agony and the ecstasy (once landed) of Jo and Ellen battling with sailfish to over 70lb and yellow-fin tuna to 50lb on just 30lb gear, plus an assortment of yellow-fin trevally and bonito. Unfortunately and except for a 350lb black marlin landed by another Hemingways boat, marlin were conspicuous by their absence during our short stay. Stewart and I however were more than kept busy in the 16-foot dinghy, sporting a 40hp outboard, exploring an assortment of known banks, drop-offs and gullies with names like Wahoo Villa, the Canyon, Karambesi Corner, the Mountains, the Nipple and the Boiling Pot, in depths ranging from 30 to over 300 feet. During our morning excursions to these evocative locations (we were back at the bar for 1p.m.) we enjoyed some cracking, arm-wrenching battles on 20lb test gear trolling size 14 CD Rapala Magnums and jigs with yellow-fin tuna to over 60lb, kingfish to 20lb, plus jumbo-sized bonito and several trevally species. My, how those yellow-fins pulled. If there is a harder, more stamina-packed saltwater species to wear down and subdue on a pound-for-pound basis, then I would dearly love to catch it.

The impressive list of blue-water monsters caught from Hemingways boats includes black marlin to 733½lb, blue marlin to 834lb, striped marlin to 197lb, sailfish to 131lb, wahoo to 101lb, giant trevally to 121lb, kingfish to 76lb, dorado to 50½lb, cobia to 73½lb, yellow-fin tuna to 192lb, bonito to 21lb, spear fish to 46lb, tiger sharks to 717lb and mako sharks to 270½lb. Visitors should note that to conserve fish stocks a tag-and-release scheme is now implemented with all marlin, sailfish and giant trevallys. An exciting option available here, incidentally, is to make an overnight trip to the famous north Kenya bank (over 50 miles out north-east of Watamu) to troll or work squid baits for the legendary broad-bill swordfish during the hours of darkness.

Kenya's coast is dominated by the twice-yearly monsoons which blow from and to the Arabian Gulf, bringing warm and light (kaskazi) north-easterly winds during the prime bill fishing period from December through till March. Sailfish however often come inshore in numbers during August and thereafter sport can either be hectic or

Above *My old mate and fellow angling journalist Dave Lewis is a regular visitor to the warm blue waters off Kenya. He caught this massive, highly prized 94lb giant trevally (also called 'karambesi' locally) using livebait whilst downrigger trolling over a deep-water bank. What a powerful scrap these members of the jack family put up.*

Previous spread *Small kona-head trolling lures are most effective for both wahoo and this stunningly coloured, some would say most beautifully painted of all pelagic species, the fast-moving and acrobatic dorado. Though also called dolphin fish, it is of course not a mammal but a true blue-water sportsfish. Eats well too. Try blackened Cajun dorado.*

Below *These silver-sided kingfish are not dissimilar to a giant mackerel and can attain weights approaching 100lb. I was more than happy with this twenty-five-pounder, supported at its munching end by Hemingway's guide, Kahindi. It gobbled up a mounted frigate mackerel on the troll. Note its distinct swallow tail and the rows of razor-sharp teeth which can slice through both fish and your fingers.*

quiet. During the rest of the year, cooler south-east (kusi) winds prevail with noticeably rougher seas. Despite this, boats at Hemingways generally fish from July through till sometime in May with the knowledge that as most pelagic species are simply passing through and not resident, catching to a timetable from one year to another is never an exact science.

The managing director of Hemingways, Garry Cullen, is a most enthusiastic host and up at the crack of dawn every morning to ensure guests enjoy a hearty breakfast and fill their lunch boxes from the cold buffet before setting offshore to do battle. Though a pro golfer for almost 20 years, angling won through in the end when Garry set up Hemingways in 1988. Now he specializes in fly rodding for the acrobatic sailfish, which lights up and changes colour from electric blues to various shades of purple during memorable fights on size 11 or 12 weight fly tackle and pinkish coloured flies up to 9 inches in length tied on a size 6/0 hook. The general technique however (though guests are encouraged to try fly rodding) is trolling at somewhere between 6 and 8 knots in these clear, warm, blue seas, anything up to 25 miles from base. Hemingways Resort is situated in the middle of a huge bay protected 400 yards out by a natural reef, providing a safe inner harbour to the dozen or so game boats anchored in the Watamu National Marine Park and Reserve. There are over 1000 species of fish and 200 types of coral to be found here in shallow, crystal-clear water, which ensures guests enjoy unparalleled snorkelling plus trips in the glass-bottomed boat to feed the friendliest of reef fishes which take bread scraps from your hand.

Left *With its athletic body charged up in iridescent shades of bronze, purple and blue, a high-leaping sail-fish catapulting itself clear of the surface is indeed a sight to behold. Some anglers, myself included, care not whether the hook stays in or is flung out so long as the sail can be 'jumped' a few times. At Hemingways, along with giant trevally and marlin, all sailfish are released.*

Above *Combining a few days game-viewing safari at the famous Masai Mara National Game Reserve is an option all anglers should consider when planning an offshore-fishing holiday at Hemingways. Visitors are transported by Land Cruisers to within close range of many animals, including cheetahs and lions at their kill, plus zebras, elephant, waterbuck, buffalo, wildebeest, hyena and giraffe.*

Other facilities organized at the resort include riding and golf, wind surfing, beach barbecues, scuba diving and dhow trips along the tranquil waters of nearby Mida Creek sipping exotic Hemingways' specials called Damas. Strangely, in Swahili this means 'medicine', and is a wonderful concoction of crushed ice, vodka, lime juice, sugar and honey.

Seafood eats cooked on board are also served during these sundowner trips which afford interesting spotting for a galaxy of wading birds working the mangrove-lined mudflats, including curlews, egrets and herons, plus ospreys and fish eagles high overhead.

When Jo and I reluctantly had to depart from Hemingways our African holiday was not entirely over. A two-hour flight from Mombasa by light aircraft took us in a north-westerly direction across the Tsavo National Park towards the famous Masai Mara National Game Reserve, with outstanding views to the south through the aircraft's windows of Africa's highest mountain, Mount Kilimanjaro, which reaches 19,304 feet. It is the eighth highest mountain in the world, heavily snow topped, and protrudes eerily through the puffy white clouds.

We had booked two days of game viewing at the Mara Safari Club set in riverine forest which has luxury tented accommodation overlooking the Mara River. All tents here boast four-poster beds, *en suite* facilities, and the decking patios overlook the river which is home to crocodiles and hippos, plus myriad colourful birds. Incidentally, if you purchase the local fishing licence, there are lungfish and clarrius catfish of

Left *Once our two wives started catching, Stewart Smalley and I couldn't prise them away from the rods at any price. Here both Ellen Smalley (standing) and my wife, Jo, are enjoying a double hook-up of sail fish. Only when the girls became physically exhausted through playing a succession of 30–50 lbs yellow fin tuna were we given a go. Huh! Stewart Smalley and skipper Ali look on from the flying bridge.*

Right *Not a regular sight at Hemingways resort these days as all marlin and sail fish are carefully released. But this 550lb black marlin unfortunately died through being 'tail wrapped' (caught around the trace) and so was brought ashore. It was in fact played for various lengths of time by all three anglers. This action plus a lost monster for Stewart all occurred during the two-day Watamu Tournament, by which time Jo and I had unfortunately returned home.*

up to 20lb to be caught in the river, with ledgered strips of raw steak or fish being favoured baits.

Visitors can make up to three game drives daily in the club's Toyota Land Cruisers which accommodate six people comfortably to view through wooded hills, across savannah and open plains. Alternatively (and you have to pay extra) you can forgo the first two drives in preference for a truly memorable flight in a hot-air balloon of about one hour's duration with outstanding views of the game beneath, finishing with a champagne sit-down bush breakfast upon landing in the middle of the Mara. This was a truly unforgettable experience and notched up untold brownie points for me with Jo, following virtually non-stop fishing at Hemingways. The game viewing was simply magical, with wildebeest, zebra, topi, impala, eland, giraffe, waterbuck, Thompsons gazelles, jackals, bat-eared foxes, buffalo, hyena, elephant, cheetahs, lions and warthogs seen on virtually every drive. It was truly amazing how close to a pride of lions guests were driven – to within just a few yards in many cases. I used up more film there than when fishing. Putting the camera down was impossible, and at times I could have done with a longer lens than my 300mm.

Another option when at the Mara is a half-day excursion to Rusinga Island at Lake Victoria on the Kenyan shoreline. A 40-minute flight by light aircraft takes you directly to Rusinga's airstrip for a morning's trolling for Nile perch, and brings you back in good time for the afternoon game drive at the Mara.

The Mara Safari Club has its own resident naturalist in the form of expat Mike Clifton whose knowledge of the area has been gleaned over 30 years, and each alternative evening there is either a slide show on local flora and fauna or tribal dancing, compliments of the tall, high-leaping Masai warriors resplendent in their traditional red cloaks.

No sooner had Jo and I returned from Kenya when an excited fax from Stewart and Ellen Smalley at Hemingways related a battle with a huge black marlin on their practice day aboard charter boat *Tarka* prior to the annual Watamu big game competition, in which Stewart went on to play and subsequently lose after a five-hour battle, a gigantic, potential world-record black marlin estimated by Callum the skipper at in excess of 1,500lb. The marlin they did eventually land however weighed 550lb and unfortunately became tail wrapped following a high jump. It was nevertheless played by Ellen for over an hour then Stewart took over for just 10 minutes, before the red wine of the previous evening got the better of him, and he handed the rod over to Phil Revett, known as the Sausage Supremo (on account of him being a well-known butcher from Wickham Market in Suffolk) who then played it for a further hour still wrapped. Unfortunately the marlin died, which resulted in this trophy shot hung from the gantry. This is not a regular practice at Hemingways nowadays I should point out, as whenever possible, catch and release is encouraged. The threesome still managed to win the Watamu Tournament, however, with over 1,000lb of yellow-fin tuna landed over the two days.

THE RED RIVER
MANITOBA, CANADA

anada is blessed with more freshwater lakes and rivers than any other country on this planet. The vastness of the arctic-like Northwest Territories alone contain nine per cent of the world's fresh water. Running a creditable second, however, is the province of Manitoba, known as the Land of a Hundred Thousand Lakes, most of which, would you believe, are unnamed. Lake Winnipeg is the eleventh largest body of fresh water in the world. Feeding Lake Winnipeg is the fabulous Red River, which originates south of the border with the United States in Minnesota (as does the Mississippi) and flows in a northerly direction through the city of Winnipeg to the heartland of Canada before entering the lake. When the Red River exits Lake Winnipeg it then becomes the Nelson River and, after passing through myriad interconnecting lakes, finally empties into Hudson Bay.

The city of Winnipeg, Manitoba's capital, offers a reflection of the province's past and future, with a diverse choice in hotels, shops and especially restaurants. It has the heritage of hundreds of years with contributions of dozens of different nationalities – kind of cosmopolitan yet cosy. Named by the Ojibwee Indians, Winnipeg translates as 'muddy waters', a perfect description of the wide and incredibly fertile Red River which is always well coloured and stuffed full of fish. The two dominating species are common carp and the hard-battling channel catfish. Both average double figures, and 20lb-plus specimens are regularly caught. Channel cats are common in the 20-25lb range and

Previous spread *Both anglers simultaneously into big carp or channel catfish is a regular occurrence in the fast, foaming waters of Lockport Bridge Dam Weir pool on the marvellous Red River, just outside the city of Winnipeg.*

Above *Yes, it's now three up. Robert Ferrario, Richard Ward (middle) and I are all into sizeable common carp, hooked float fishing a shallow drainage channel.*

there is a fair sprinkling of lunkers topping 30lb. Also present are small bullhead catfish, goldeye (a roach-like fish and prime catfish bait), white bass, walleye and saugers (both similar to our zander), pike, freshwater drum which can weigh 5-15lb, and the very occasional white sturgeon to over 100lb.

From the northern suburbs of Winnipeg, covering a distance of some 30 miles all the way down to Lake Winnipeg, the Red River is joined by a massive interconnecting network of creeks, drainage channels, rivers and lakes, with marvellous fishing throughout. The very finest, most unbelievably fish-packed location of all, however, is immediately downstream of the St. Andrew's huge dam and weir at Lockport Bridge, just an hour's drive from Winnipeg Airport. Incidentally, the best way of getting here is a nine-hour flight from Heathrow to Minneapolis, followed by just an hour's internal flight to Winnipeg. The man who makes it all happen along this unique river is my old friend, hunter and fishing guide, Stu Mckay, who runs Cats on the Red, a comprehensive outfitters comprising tackle and bait shop, boat hiring (18-foot customized aluminium boats), launching and guiding service, plus comfortable self-catering cabin-type accommodation – all situated within a short cast of the Red River, a few hundred yards downriver from the weir.

Throughout the 1990s, when making international television programmes or whilst escorting parties of specimen hunters from the UK, I cannot think of a day when Stu hasn't made it happen for me on the Red. His knowledge of the system is truly second to none. He even provides free bait to carp enthusiasts in the way of 'Stu's stinking corn'. The recipe is simple. A sack of hard, dry maize is emptied into a large plastic bin and covered in boiling water. Several bags of sugar are then stirred in. The mixture is then left to ferment for several weeks, whereupon, hey presto, it becomes carp bait *par excellence*. It really does stink and hasn't really softened much, and you need a long-handled ladle for obtaining a bucketful from the fermenting bin for a day's carping, and to propel loose feed out into the river. But I guarantee you'll fancy trying this great bait on your return to the UK where it works just as well. Whether I'm float fishing or bolt rig ledgering, I present three or four grains on a ¾-inch long hair rig to a size 8 hook, a 10-12lb reel line being quite sufficient.

Many visitors from the UK pile in the boilies just as they would for carp back home, and of course Red River carp quickly respond. But really stinking corn, simple pastes or even plain old breadflake is all you need in most situations. There are simply so many carp in the system – all beautiful, fully-scaled commons – and they are far from shy. There are plenty of bank-fishing spots within sight of the accommodation, or you can ask Stu to show you one of the many creeks, drainage channels or lakes connected to the Red River system. Everywhere is just stuffed with carp. At the huge dam and weir, some 300 yards across and between 15 to 24 feet deep, there is a fish ladder which during the summer months is so full of carp working their way upriver, you could walk across their backs. These are long, wonderfully proportioned common carp to 30lb plus, most of which have never seen a baited hook as few local or visiting American anglers ever try to catch them. They prefer to anchor in the swirling waters of the weir pool hooking into walleyes or saugers averaging 2-3lb apiece hooked on lures (because they

Left top *This deep-bodied and exceptionally hard-fighting species is a freshwater drum, which are common in the 6-10lb range. We caught them on breadflake and on fish cutlets of goldeye intended for channel cats.*

Left bottom *Stan Povey from the UK couldn't be dragged away from the stamp of beautifully scaled common carp displayed here. They were simply queuing up for ledgered corn or breadflake in the well-oxygenated water of Lockport Bridge Dam weir, and most were between 12 and 20lb. What marvellous fishing in addition to the unbelievable head of channel cats.*

Above *I found watching these white pelicans fish absolutely fascinating. Suddenly they would all form a large circle and start working their wings and beaks to disorientate any shoal of small bait fish below. Then it was bottoms up as they enjoyed a feeding mêlée.*

like eating them) than getting their string well and truly pulled by great big commons or catfish. And talking of cats, in the deep, swirling undercurrents of the weir's churning white water also live a truly phenomenal head of channel cats.

The ideal tackle combination, as it is throughout the Red, is a 9-10-foot heavy spinning rod (a 2½lb test curve carp rod is perfect) coupled to a 6500 sized multiplier loaded with 15lb test mono. Incidentally what I most like about channel cats is that you don't need to lose any sleep to catch them. They will bite throughout the day except in the very hottest of weather during July and early August, which leaves the evenings free to watch the sun go down over the river from the balcony of your cabin or join in the camp fire cook-outs and sing songs beside the river for which Stu and his friends are renowned. Safari atmosphere is not common to Africa alone.

Anchoring up in any likely spot will take channel cats eventually, or you can vastly improve the odds by first locating a concentration on the boat's fish finder. Then anchor up and ledger downstream. The best bait is a ½-inch-wide cutlet from a freshly killed goldeye, which are easily caught on waggler tackle back at Stu's boat dock. There is a single rod only and barbless hook rule in force throughout the province, so the barb must be crunched down before slipping the point of a wide-gape 4/0 just beneath the skin at one end. A 2-foot hook length of 25lb test will help withstand abrasion from the channel cat's two gripping pads, situated top and bottom inside the cavernous mouth. A simple running 1-2oz bomb and bead set-up above the trace swivel complete the rig.

Action with cats, as with carp, can occur all the way downstream from the white waters of the dam weir, with depths varying from 10 to over 20 feet and the bottom

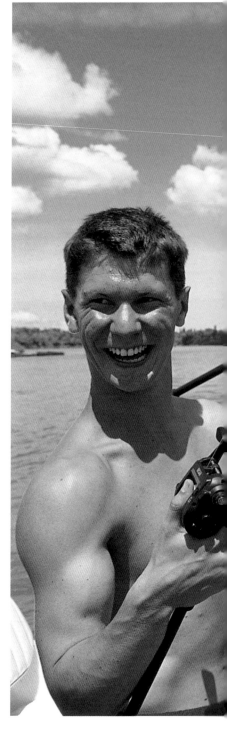

consisting of large rocks and hard clay. A peculiarity of the channel cat is that it will all too quickly drop the bait should it feel undue resistance, so it pays to allow a couple of yards of line to be taken freely, before putting the reel into gear and striking hard. I much prefer to hold the rod throughout and feel for that initial, often gentle mouthing of the goldeye cutlet, then point the rod at the fish to minimize resistance as it moves off.

Channel cats have a smooth, grey, scaleless body with huge, powerful fins (except for the tiny dorsal) and a nicely-forked proper tail. They come equipped with eight sensory whiskers to feel their way around in search of small- to medium-sized shoal fishes – four under the chin and four on top of their head, the outside two being the longest. In cross section their body is immensely thick, so the angler is usually pleasantly surprised when his trophy catch weighs considerably more than first estimated. The world record for the species, incidentally, is 50lb plus. The chances of catching the bigger fish are best during June and again during late August and through September, although channel cats bite soon after ice-out in May and continue well into October. The Red River then becomes totally frozen over all winter through.

Other likely customers, when offering goldeye cutlets on the riverbed intended for channel cats, are bullheads, which can become a nuisance at times, and the powerful

Previous spread and above
What a klonker! My old mate Stu McKay, who literally makes everything happen on the Red River, gives a happy Richard Ward from the UK a helping hand with a near-30lb channel catfish. Note the long whiskers, tiny dorsal fin, scaleless

body and proper forked tail. Pound for pound I rate them livelier and certainly more powerful fighters than carp of equal size.

Above left *Catfish bait supreme – cutlets of freshly killed goldeye, gently nicked onto a barbless 4/0 hook.*

freshwater drum. I rate this silver-sided, deep-bodied species, particularly when they are averaging 6-8lb plus, very highly indeed and enjoy their dogged fight immensely. Stu actually specializes in catching drum on the fly whenever the river is less coloured. What marvellous scraps he must have.

LAKE VICTORIA
AND THE RIVER NILE
UGANDA

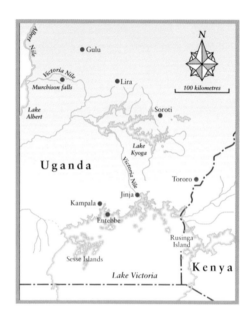

In his fascinating book *Journey to the Source of the Nile*, adventurer Christopher Ondaatje retraces and travels the exact routes taken by Victorian, British-born explorers in their quest to unravel the mystery of the source of the planet's longest river. Various theses have been put forward by the likes of Grant, Baker, Burton, Henry Moreton Stanley and, of course, Dr. David Livingstone during their hazardous expeditions between 1856 and 1877, and each differed enormously. Was Lake Tanganyika the Nile's source or maybe Lake Albert, fed by the Semliki River? Perhaps the source waters of this majestic river were initiated by the Ruwenzori Mountains? Or is it simply the obvious answer (and incidentally the conclusion to which Christopher Ondaatje's book points the reader) that Lake Victoria itself is the source of the Nile?

Previous spread *Beside overhanging canopies of vines and tall hardwood trees full of monkeys and exotic birds, guide Paul Goldring (centre) steers the boat along a steep-sided drop-off in the Sesse Islands waiting for Nile perch to grab one of the lures. On the left is Jonathan Wright of Semliki Safaris and on the right fellow angling journalist Dave Lewis. Nail-biting trolling this, where any second the rod could be wrenched over and produce a new world record. Lesser achievements, Nile perch weighing over 100lb for instance, are weekly occurrences.*

Left *Nile perch do everything they can to rid themselves of the lure, rushing to the surface in a head-shaking, tail-walking display. Not the kind of antics most anglers expect from such portly species, following their typical deep-down, dogged way of fighting.*

Right *Yes, white-knuckle time indeed and the moment of truth as a 90lb Sesse Islands Nile perch comes crashing out, its huge mouth wide open. Fortunately the hooks on my medium-sized green Russelure held and the fish was released to fight another day. Note how I prefer to keep the rod bent on a leaping fish. If it goes slack, the weight of the lure is not supported and is more easily shaken out.*

Starting a little south of Jinga at what was once Ripon Falls, now swallowed from view by the Owen Falls Dam situated further downstream north of the town, the Victoria Nile cuts north-east, first over Karuma Falls, through Chobe and on to Murchison Falls, then down to Lake Albert where it is called the Albert Nile. Upon leaving the Lake it eventually becomes the White Nile and flows north to Omdurman, near Khartoum, in the Sudan where it joins forces with the Blue Nile, which originates in Ethiopia. This truly majestic river continues in a northerly direction and flows into what is now massive Lake Nasser in Egypt then on to Luxor and Cairo, finally emptying its mysteries into the Mediterranean Sea. Oh how I wish I had another lifetime in which to explore this magnificent, enigmatic river. How can anyone even begin to scratch the surface along a watercourse that exceeds 4,000 miles in length? Didn't most of our Victorian explorers die in the attempt?

But let's first consider the enormity of Lake Victoria itself, so named in 1858 by intrepid explorer John Hanning Speke. It is a sheet of stillwater, second only in size to Lake Superior, and amounting to 26,800 square miles of fishing potential containing more than a thousand tropical islands from just a few acres in size to some of 150 square miles. Its overall magnitude can in fact be compared with the landmass of Ireland. What a truly phenomenal freshwater fishery and home, as many believe, to the most monstrous Nile perch in the entirety of Africa. There are also whitefish, catfish and several species of tilapia present. The bird life is unbelievably prolific and diverse, and

there is always a chance of seeing the occasional pod of hippos or the spotted-necked otter, which is thought to be unique to Lake Victoria. Even more incredible is that, prior to 1954, Nile perch were not found above Murchison Falls (although scientific evidence of fossils disputes this) when just seven perch were transferred by the then game warden, Bruce Kinlock, and carried up the steep escarpment in a galvanized bath tub and released into the Upper Nile. Apparently further stockings were made over the next four years before the programme was discontinued because it was found that perch could ascend into Lake Victoria through the turbines of the Owen Falls Dam. Recent studies indicate the Nile perch now constitutes 80 per cent of the fish population in Lake Victoria. So exactly who do you believe?

Left *This trio of monster perch caught by Norfolk anglers Jim and Linda Tyree, trolling out from Rusinga Island, weighed a staggering 112lb, 127lb and 154lb respectively. Jim was rather perplexed and unhappy about the Lodge's policy of killing all Nile perch caught. They were, however, distributed between and eaten by local people. Dare I say 'when in Rome'!*

Right *There are many delights to be seen on Lake Victoria whilst trolling over sunken plateaux and around unspoilt tropical islands. My favourite is watching the brown and white African fish eagle extend its talons and at phenomenal speed lift sizeable fish from the surface. You can literally hear the power in its wings as it takes off.*

Three countries meet around the shoreline of Lake Victoria: Tanzania, Uganda and Kenya, whose ownership of the north-east corner is by far the smallest. Actually it was in Kenya on beautiful Rusinga Island, during the shooting of a 12-part world-wide series of my Anglia Television programme *Go Fishing*, where I first experienced the thrill of trolling for the legendary Nile perch back in the early 1990s. I have been both fascinated and excited by the species ever since.

The lodge at Rusinga Island is where anglers stay on the Kenyan shoreline, though many visitors including even non-anglers, are flown in by light aircraft on a daily basis for just a morning's trolling whilst on safari at the famous Masai Mara National Game Reserve. Such was the experience shared by my good friends Jim and Linda Tyree, who were on safari at the time and who jumped at the chance of a morning's Nile perch fishing. In fact I asked Jim for some advice about the species prior to my first visit. His answer was, 'we only had four hits, resulting in three perch each over 100lb apiece, plus another missed, then it was time to come in for lunch'. Jim incidentally was none too pleased about the policy of killing everything caught, but their trio of monstrous perch to 150lb illustrates just how prolific this area was at that time.

I nevertheless have some wonderful memories of perch caught over several years fishing out from Rusinga Island. Each day's trolling around the neighbouring islands resulted in a plethora of hard-battling, head-shaking, acrobatic perch in the 20-50lbs

size bracket, plus a fair sprinkling of whoppers. However at the time I too questioned the management about their policy (it may well now have altered) of killing every perch landed.

My pal Andy Davison, once held the IGFA Nile perch world record with a mammoth 191½ lb fish caught trolling a gold Russelure out from Rusinga, and there were several unratified monsters caught exceeding 200lb. A colossal perch of 416lb commercially netted from Lake Victoria is actually mentioned in the *Guinness Book of Records*. So it is indeed anyone's guess as to what the optimum weight of this magnificent species really is.

Throughout the 1990s, however, along with commercial fishing for perch escalating to an all-time high within the Kenyan sector, sportsfishing potential started noticeably to spiral downwards. We all trotted out the old adage that you can't tell a local to put back a food fish in a Third World country, which, of course, is perfectly true. But then what is also true is that the golden goose can lay only so many eggs and I rather fancy that in the long run the local guide who helps tourists land and return their catches year after year will always enjoy food in his belly and reap a high standard of living.

At the time of writing, to the best of my knowledge, there are no lodges nor much of an infrastructure to arrange any kind of sportsfishing safari from the Tanzanian part of the lake which staggeringly amounts to over half, but I am certain one day it will all open up. For the present the best sportsfishing area lies in the Ugandan sector around the beautiful Sesse Islands. This is an interesting group of 84 islands, bisected by the

Above *For every huge crocodile you can see basking above the surface like this near-twenty-footer, there might be fifty below which you cannot. Anglers bank fishing from rocky ledges into the swirling torrential currents of the Nile at Murchison Falls can never contemplate a quick dip to cool off. Falling in would mean an almost certain horrid death.*

Left *No wonder fishing buddy Dave Lewis and guide George look pleased. This superbly proportioned 40lb-plus bagras catfish (called* sementendu *locally) snuffed up Dave's ledgered small tiger fish deadbait from the bottom of a thirty-feet deep eddy in the slower water immediately downstream from majestic Murchison Falls. The Nile is both bountiful and dangerous in these parts.*

equator, only the largest of which has any substantial development. The area is an unspoilt tropical haven full of monkeys and exotic birds, from paradise fly catchers to giant kingfishers, where dense canopies of vines and tall hardwood trees overhang the steep-sided shorelines providing perches to fish eagles, kites and buzzards. As you troll diving lures on 30lb-class gear along the steep drop-offs, giant monitor lizards and the occasional python can be seen basking on the marginal rocks. What's more, the Sesse Islands are easily accessible, being just 20 miles south of Entebbe in the lake's north-western corner with direct eight-hour flights from Heathrow. It is then but a 90-minute boat trip and you are at the sandy shore (good fly fishing for immature perch and tilapia) of the Islands Club on Kalangala Island whose management cater especially for anglers.

There is a tremendous concentration of Nile perch in the 10-20lb range around the Sesse Islands. There are enough between 40 and 80lb to satisfy the experienced perch enthusiast, with 100lb-plus bulls turning up most weeks. A new world record is quite literally just around the corner and could well be your next fish. In commercial nets Ugandan Nile perch have been recorded to close on 400lb. On rod and line a 251 pounder caught trolling only half a mile offshore from Entebbe in 1998 by Mr Savel Du Plessi (though not claimed) is the heaviest in recent years. It is all waiting to happen.

Nile perch safaris to these wonderful islands are arranged by Paul Goldring of G & C Tours based in Entebbe. Through Wild Frontiers, which encompasses both

photographic game viewing and fishing expeditions, Paul has twice guided me around these Sesse Islands. Our deep-diving Russelures, Rapalas and Manns 25 (Paul's favourite big perch lure) trolled at around two knots soon attracted perch. Fellow angling journalist Dave Lewis caught his first Nile perch, a plump, high-leaping 50 pounder. I banged into a 90 pounder. Christine Slater boated a deep-bellied specimen of almost 80lb and Brian Garnett of Barnet sickened us all by landing a goliath of 143lb on only his second day out perching – by far his largest fish ever.

After a whirlwind tour, including many more perch, we were on our way back to Entebbe for an hour's flight by light aircraft (it is a six-hour drive by Land Rover) to one of the world's most spectacular freshwater locations situated in the Murchison Falls National Park. Due to the manner in which the entire might of the River Nile pours through a twisting fissure in the escarpment of rocks just six yards wide, before tumbling 150 feet below into a foaming maelstrom of churning white water, Murchison Falls – named by the explorer Baker, after Sir Roderick Murchison, the then president of the Royal Geographical Society – is truly one of the most awesome fishing locations it has every been my privilege to behold, let alone fish. I first became mesmerized by their splendour during my youth whilst watching that marvellous motion picture of the 1950s, *King Solomon's Mines* starring Stewart Granger and Deborah Kerr. Little did I know then that one day I would be standing on those very same rocks to hear the thunder of the Nile and better still be working lures and livebaits into the dark, mysterious waters in search of monster perch.

Beneath an unbelievably complex pattern of eddies, fast runs and cross currents, which seem to alter direction every few minutes, in the gigantic pool which is up to 400 yards across and extends for fully half a mile downstream, live two hard-fighting species of catfish (the sementendu-bagras and the vundu) both of which reach weights in excess of 100lb apiece, plus the Nile perch itself. The largest in recent years has been a titanic specimen of 237lb caught by local expert Marco Magyar. There are, of course, numerous other exotic, extremely colourful species inhabiting this part of the Nile, including the black-spotted electric catfish, squeeker catfish, elephant snout fish, several labeo-barbel types, plus tiger fish, awakas and alestes – the last three being by far the best baits for a big perch or catfish.

To fish here visitors have the option of staying above the falls at the Sambiya River Lodge, situated just 20 minutes away by road in a setting of Savannah plain and riverine forest with superb game viewing close by, but with a steep, arduous walk down and up again each day to reach fishable levels. Alternatively you can stay downstream at the highly acclaimed Sarova Paraa Lodge on the north bank opposite the ferry crossing at Paraa, or at the Nile Safari Camp situated further downstream on the southern bank and then take the 25-foot fishing boat Mamba upstream to the falls. On the way close, visual encounters with numerous pods of hippos and massive crocodiles are guaranteed. Other likely sightings are elephant, buffalo, wart hogs, baboons, waterbuck, giraffes and myriad birds from pelicans and fish eagles to the rare shoebill stork. Here the Nile splits around long islands of weed and papyrus and is up to 500 yards wide. It is a totally fascinating journey.

On my last visit in March 2000 the fishing was outstanding. As water levels were extremely low I was able to worm myself through a mass of gnarled tree roots around the steep-sided ledges into the most upstream pool of the falls, the Devil's Cauldron itself. This is pretty dangerous, to say the least, because should you fall in and not be able to scramble out, half a mile downriver are some of the largest, meanest crocodiles on this planet, just waiting for an easy meal to drift by – something of which guide, Paul Goldring, took great delight in reminding me, whenever we momentarily lost our footing.

The previous evening I had made up a huge ball of fresh bread paste so that our local guide, George, could provide me with a regular supply of livebaits in the way of alestes (also catchable on small spinners). After taking several perch in the 20-40lb range, I became connected with a truly monstrous specimen. This particular fish engulfed my 1½ lb freelined livebait and, upon feeling cold steel, stripped off over 100 yards of 35 lb test as it charged across the football pitch-sized pool of the Devil's Cauldron. Despite grating over huge boulders on the riverbed, the line held allowing me to witness a goliath perch well in excess of 100lb (possibly closer to 200lb) lunge across the foam-filled pool, as they characteristically do in order to shake the hook free, before diving deep and returning to more or less the same spot where I first hooked it, close to the bottom of a deep eddy immediately behind a partly-submerged rocky outcrop. I had a ten-minute scrap of pure joy, but the monster was nowhere near finished. Then quite inexplicably, as it prepared itself for another circuit of the pool, the size 8/0 hook fell out and I reeled in a badly frayed slack line. An hour or so later I was to experience a similar fight, only this time the perch managed to rip the line to shreds over the rocks on its initial run. The Devil's Cauldron, indeed the entirety of Murchison Falls, does not give up its monsters easily. But where else can you stand perched on rocks in such a wonderfully hostile yet beautiful environment as that of Murchison Gorge? You feel the intense daytime heat, suppressed by thunderous spray on your face, and stand a very real chance of hooking into the next world record of no fewer than three separate species, while egrets and hammercops explore the foamy shoreline and high overhead in the thermals yellow-billed kites and fish eagles survey the rapids below for an easy meal.

I did eventually land a superb vundu catfish of around 60lb from the Devil's Cauldron late in the afternoon of that very same day when the livebaits had run out. It grabbed a sinking depth raider plug cast fully 50 yards into the foaming white water beneath the main run and led me a real song and dance through and around the rocks, before I was able to get it under control. Incidentally, I rate depth raiders, both floating and sinking, and the Rapala sinking CD18 plugs by far the most effective lures for Murchison Falls. And as with livebaiting a monofilament reel line of 30-35lb test is imperative. My standard freshwater big fish outfit consists of a Masterline 9½-foot Voyager rod and ABU 10000 multiplier, which fits the bill admirably throughout African and Indian freshwaters.

On other occasions, when concentrating on some of the deep, slower eddies (which shelve to 30 feet plus) whilst boat fishing from Mamba at the very tail end of the long pool, I was actually able to work a livebait close to the bottom using a sliding (through the middle) pike float rig. And boy did I get a fright when on a couple of occasions within just three to four feet of the float a hippo's huge head suddenly erupted from the surface in a loud snort of spray. I couldn't wind the line quick enough because the last thing any fisherman needs on the end of his line is a foul-hooked hippo, believe me. Also irritating, though perhaps a novelty initially, are the bait-robbing, soft-shelled turtles which have a nasty habit of snagging you amongst the rocks.

After experimenting with several terminal rigs including a large single hook in the bait's lip and not being very happy about control or hook-ups, I settled for a treble and single hook combo tied 5 inches apart on a 4-foot 100lb-test mono trace, in order to avoid chafing from the rough gripping pads, abrasive lips and gill plates of the Nile perch. One prong of the 5/0 treble was set into the livebait's top lip and the 8/0 single

gently nicked beneath its dorsal root. I found that whether float fishing or freelining, which is perhaps the most effective technique overall for both perch and catfish (because the bait seeks to swim deep down between the rocks), having the top hook in the dorsal usually kept the bait working downwards. Whereas if it was hooked in the top lip only any kind of control immediately steered the bait upwards and away from the strike zones. All that was needed was gentle thumb control on the reel spool as the bait swam off to ensure it dived deeply down away from the boat or rocky fishing ledges, long casting being completely unnecessary. And there was certainly no mistaking hits from either perch or catfish, with the line suddenly evaporating from the reel at speed and the rod tip pulling over firmly.

In my capacity as both angling journalist and television producer/presenter it has been my good fortune to sample exotic sportsfishing locations in many of the world's most spectacular tropical destinations. But none, and I do mean none, can compare with the inspirational majesty, the breathtaking scenery, the raw, untamed awesome beauty and yes, even the hard-biting tsetse flies of Murchison Falls. If you are an angler you will feel as though you have returned to the womb. These falls are indeed Uganda's Cauldron of the Gods.

Above *This aerial shot I took from a light aircraft way above Murchison Falls shows how the full might and width of the River Nile is forced through a narrow twisting fissure in the rocks mere yards wide, to fall 150 feet below into a churning, foaming maelstrom of white water. Measuring up to 400 yards across, the resulting pool roars downstream for a distance of over half a mile through a steep gorge completely overgrown with tropical vegetation. There is a narrow path here, however, along the southern ridge for those wishing to explore a succession of mouth watering lies.*

*And here is the awesome scene
anglers who climb to the end of
that path will experience: the
Devil's Cauldron itself! I
personally have seen no other pool
to compare nor wetted a line in
anywhere near so evocative or so
spiritually inspiring in all my
travels. But I shall keep looking.*

USEFUL DESTINATION AND ITINERARY NOTES

MALARIA AND INOCULATIONS

Malaria is endemic in many areas of the world and you should always seek the advice of a qualified medical practitioner when you are planning a trip abroad. Courses of anti-malarial tablets should be started prior to departure (and continued after your return), so ensure you consult your doctor in good time. Other inoculations may be demanded by the country you are visiting before you are permitted entry. There are also a number of inoculations that, although not compulsory, you might be advised to have. The inoculations listed in Destination Facts and Requirements should be used as guidelines only.

DESTINATION FACTS AND REQUIREMENTS

LAKE NASSER, EGYPT

Safari organizer on the lake:	**Tim Baily** The African Angler P.O.Box191 Aswan, Egypt tel: (20) 97 316052 fax: (20) 97 310907 mobile: (20) 101342401 e-mail: aangler@sofitcom.com.eg
UK booking agents/ tour operators	**Tailor Made Holidays** 5 Station Approach Hinchley Wood Surrey KT10 0SP tel: (0208) 398 0188 fax: (0208) 398 6007 e-mail: chris@tailormadeholidays.co.uk
	Safari Plus 34 Dene Street Dorking Surrey RH4 2DB tel/fax: (01306) 883204 mobile: 0585 755013

Airlines:	British Airways and Egypt Air (Heathrow–Luxor–Aswan)
Suggested inoculations:	Anti-malarial tablets, tetanus, hepatitis A, typhoid, polio
Egyptian currency:	5 Egyptian pounds to £1 sterling
Fishing licences:	Obtainable through safari organizer
Passport/visas:	10-year passport (valid 6 months) and visa required. Visas obtainable on arrival in Egypt

THE BEAUTIFUL BAHAMAS

Lodge and guiding availability:	**Bahamas Ministry of Tourism** PO Box N-3701 Nassau Bahamas tel: (242) 322 7500 fax: (242) 328 0945 website: www.bahamas.com

UK Bahamas Tourist Office
3 The Billings
Walnut Tree Close
Guildford
Surrey GU1 4UL
tel: (01483) 448900
fax: (01483) 571846

UK booking agents/ tour operators:	**Go Fishing World-wide** 2 Oxford House 24 Oxford Road North London W4 4DH tel: (0208) 742 1556 fax: (0208) 747 4331 e-mail: maggi@gofishing.demon.co.uk website: www.gofishing-world-wide.com

Tailor Made Holidays
5 Station Approach
Hinchley Wood
Surrey KT10 0SP
tel: (0208) 398 0188
fax: (0208) 398 6007
e-mail: chris@tailormadeholidays.co.uk

Airlines:	British Airways (Heathrow–Nassau) American Airways and Virgin Atlantic (Gatwick/Heathrow–Miami) Bahamasair (21 destinations within the Bahamas from and to Miami and Nassau, tel: (800) 222 4262)
Suggested inoculations:	Yellow fever, only if arriving from an infected country
Bahamian currency:	Based on and almost equivalent to the US dollar. Approx. $1.40 Bahamian dollars to £1 sterling
Fishing licences:	None required
Passport/visas:	Passport required. No visa needed

THE GAMBIA, WEST AFRICA

Charter fishing boats **Gambia Fishing**
based at Denton Mark Longster and Tracey Day
Road Bridge, Banjul: tel: 00 220 495683
e-mail: Gambiafishing@hotmail.com
website: www.tarpon.co.uk

UK booking agents/ **World Sport Fishing**
tour operators: Tythe Farm
Wyboston
Bedfordshire MK44 3AT
tel: (01480) 403293
fax: (01480) 403296
e-mail: rswsf@aol.com
website: www.worldsportfishing.com

The Gambia Experience
Kingfisher House
Rownhams Lane
North Baddesley
Hampshire SO42 9LP
tel: (023) 8073 0888
fax: (023) 8073 1122
e-mail: holidays@gambia.co.uk
website: www.gambia.co.uk

Jackie Day
170 Fairway Road
Shepshed
Loughborough
Lincolnshire LE12 9HQ
tel: (01509) 506887

Airlines: Monarch (charter flights,
Gatwick–Banjul)

Suggested Anti-malarial tablets, tetanus,
inoculations: hepatitis A, yellow fever, polio, typhoid

Gambian currency: Approx. 20 dalaises to £1 sterling

Fishing licences: None required

Passport/visas: 10-year passport (valid 6 months).
No visa needed

THE FRASER RIVER, BRITISH COLUMBIA, CANADA

Organizer on **Fred's Fishing Adventures**
the river: Unit 1, 5580 Vedder Road
Chilliwack,   British Columbia
Canada V2R 5P4
tel: (604) 858 7344
fax: (604) 858 7307
e-mail: helmerjr@uniserve.com
website: http://www.freds-bc.com

UK booking agents/ **Tailor Made Holidays**
tour operators: 5 Station Approach
Hinchley Wood
Surrey KT10 0SP
tel: (0208) 398 0188
fax: (0208) 398 6007
e-mail: chris@tailormadeholidays.co.uk

Airlines: British Airways and Air Canada
(Heathrow –Vancouver, then 2-hour
road transfer)

Suggested None
inoculations:

Canadian currency:	Canadian $2.20 to £1 sterling
Fishing licences:	Obtainable through organizer and registered guides
Passport/visas:	10-year passport (valid 6 months). No visa needed

NAMIBIA'S SKELETON COAST, AFRICA

Beach fishing safari organizer in Swakopmund:	**Ottmar Leippert** Levo Sportsfishing PO Box 1860 Longbeach Walvis Bay Namibia tel/fax: (09264) 64207555
UK booking agents/ tour operators:	**Safari Plus** 34 Dene Street Dorking Surrey RH4 2DB tel/fax: (01306) 883204 mobile: 0585 755013
	Tailor Made Holidays 5 Station Approach Hinchley Wood Surrey KT10 0SP tel: (0208) 398 0188 fax: (0208) 398 6007 e-mail: chris@tailormadeholidays.co.uk
Airlines:	Air Namibia (Heathrow–Windhoek, then 5-hour car transfer to Swakopmund)

Suggested inoculations:	Anti-malarial tablets
Namibian currency:	Namibian $10.50 to £1 sterling
Fishing licences:	None required
Passport/visas:	10-year passport (valid 6 months). No visa needed

THE CAUVERY RIVER, SOUTH INDIA

Fishing safari organizers at the river (December-April):	**M/S Wildlife Association of South India** 17/1 Victoria Road Bangalore 560047 South India tel: (080) 5300378
	M/S Jungle Lodges and Resorts Ltd 2nd floor, Shrungar Shopping Centre M.G. Road Bangalore 560001 South India tel: (080) 5597021/4/5 fax: (080) 5586163 e-mail: junglelodges@vsnl.com website: www.junglelodges.com
UK booking agents/ tour operators:	**Chandertal Tours** 20 The Fridays East Dean, nr Eastbourne East Sussex BN20 0DH tel: 01323 422213 email: chandertal.tours@btinternet.com website: chandertal-tours.freeserve.co.uk/

Airlines:	Air India (Heathrow–Bangalore, 3 times weekly)	UK booking agents/ tour operators:	**John Rawle** Florida Keys Fishing Holidays 'Bellropes' Maldon Road Bradwell-on-Sea Essex CM0 7HY tel: (01621) 776445 mobile: 0860 920964
Suggested inoculations:	Anti-malarial tablets, tetanus, hepatitis A, polio, typhoid, diphtheria		
Indian currency:	65 rupees to £1 sterling		
Fishing licences:	From organizers at the river	Airlines:	American Airlines and Virgin Atlantic (Gatwick–Miami)
Passport/visas:	10-year passport (valid 6 months) and 3-month visa required, obtainable in advance from Indian High Commission, London (tel: (0207) 8368484) or send passport plus two photos plus fee to Benmar Limited, Passport Services, 12 Henrietta Street, Covent Garden, London WC2E 8LH (tel: (0207) 379 6418) who arrange visa and return stamped passport within 4 days	Suggested innoculations:	None required
		American currency:	US $1.50 to £1 sterling
		Fishing licences:	None required if fishing on charter boat or with local guides, or with Florida resident. Otherwise, licences available from Post Offices and tackle shops
		Passport/visas:	Passport only required (valid 3 months)

ISLAMORADA, FLORIDA KEYS, UNITED STATES

Organizers in The Keys:	**Bud 'n' Mary's Fishing Marina** PO Box 628, Mile Marker 79.5 Islamorada, Florida Keys 33036 USA tel: (305) 664 2461
	The Dockmaster's Office Whale Harbour Marina PO Box 1502 Islamorada, Florida USA tel: (305) 664 4511

THE ZAMBEZI RIVER AND LAKE KARIBA OF ZAMBIA AND ZIMBABWE

Fishing safari organizers in Zambia and Zimbabwe:

Zambia:	**The Royal Zambezi Lodge** Lower Zambezi Chiawa, Zambia

Information:	PO Box 33
	111 Lusaka
	tel: 274901

Zimbabwe:	**Ichingo Chobe River Lodge**
	PO Box 55
	Kasawe
	Botswana
	tel: (267) 650143
	fax: (267) 650223
	e-mail: inchingo@iafrica.com

Imbabala Safari Camp
PO Box 159
Victoria Falls
Zimbabwe
tel: 13 2004

Lake Kariba:	**Breeze's Boats**
	Marineland Harbour
	Kariba
	Zimbabwe

Fishing Safaris
Marineland Harbour
Box 62
Kariba
Zimbabwe
tel: 2419

UK booking agents/	**Tailor Made Holidays**
tour operators:	5 Station Approach
	Hinchley Wood
	Surrey KT10 0SP
	tel: (0208) 398 0188
	fax: (0208) 398 6007
	e-mail: chris@tailormadeholidays.co.uk

Safari Plus
34 Dene Street
Dorking
Surrey RH4 2DB
tel/fax: (01306) 883204
mobile: 0585 755013

| Airlines: | British Airways |
| | (Gatwick–Harare–Lusaka) |

| Suggested inoculations: | Anti-malarial tablets, tetanus, hepatitis A, diphtheria, typhoid, polio |

| Zambian currency: | 5000 kwacha to £1 sterling |

| Zimbabwean currency: | 80 Zimbabwean dollars to £1 sterling |

| Fishing licences: | Permits must be obtained in advance when fishing in the Sanyati Gorge on Lake Kariba, available at the gorge entrance. Otherwise none required on lake and river |

| Passport/visas: | Visa required for Zambia only, obtainable at Lusaka Airport. Otherwise 10-year passport (valid 6 months) |

Rio Ebro and Rio Segre, Spain

Organizers for	**Bavarian Guiding Service**
Mequinenza	Weinbergstrausse 13 89349
Fishing Camp:	Burtenbach,
	Germany
	tel: 082885/475
	fax: 08285/928077
	e-mail: infor@bavarian-guiding-service.de.internet
	website: www.bavarian-guiding-service.de

**Mequinenza Fishing Camp
in Spain**
tel/fax: 9 7446 5032

UK booking agents/ tour operators:	**Keith Lambert** 8 Booths Close Welham Green Hertfordshire AL9 7NW tel/fax: (01707) 272269
Airlines:	Iberia Airlines (Heathrow–Barcelona) Easyjet (Luton–Barcelona, then car hire, 1.5-hour drive)
Suggested innoculations:	None
Spanish currency:	1.6 euros to £1 sterling
Fishing licences:	Must be booked well in advance through fishing camp organizers
Passport/visas:	10-year passport (valid 6 months)

WATAMU, KENYA

Fishing trips at Watamu:	**Hemingways Resort** PO Box 267 Watamu Kenya tel: (254) 122 32624 fax: (254) 122 32256 e-mail: hemingways@form-net.com website: www.hemingways.co.ke

UK booking agents/ tour operators:	**Tailor Made Holidays** 5 Station Approach Hinchley Wood Surrey KT10 0SP tel: (0208) 398 0188 fax: (0208) 398 6007 e-mail: chris@tailormadeholidays.co.uk
Airlines:	British Airways (Gatwick–Nairobi–Mombasa, then 2-hour road transfer)
Suggested inoculations:	Anti-malarial tablets, tetanus, diphtheria, hepatitis A, polio, typhoid
Kenyan currency:	105 Kenyan shillings to £1 sterling
Fishing licences:	Only required to fish inland at the Mara River if on safari at the Mara Safari Club
Passport/visas:	10-year passport (valid 6 months)

THE RED RIVER, MANITOBA, CANADA

Organizer on the river:	**Stu McKay Outfitters** 'Cats on the Red' G.D. Station Lockport Manitoba R1A 3RP Canada tel/fax: (204) 757 9876

UK booking agents/ *tour operators:*	**Tailor Made Holidays** 5 Station Approach Hinchley Wood Surrey KT10 0SP tel: (0208) 398 0188 fax: (0208) 398 6007 e-mail: chris@tailormadeholidays.co.uk		**Semliki Safari Lodge and Safaris** PO Box 23825 Kampala Uganda tel/fax: 25641 266682 e-mail: gwg@swiftuganda.com

Airlines: North West Airlines
(Gatwick–Minneapolis–Winnipeg)

Murchison Falls Fishing Safaris
with Marco Magyar
PO Box 27752
Kampala
Uganda
tel/fax: (256) 41 286396
e-mail: bananaboat@infocom.co.ug

Canadian currency: Canadian $1.40 to £1 sterling

Fishing licences: Obtainable from Stu Mckay Outfitters

Passport/visas: 10-year passport (valid 6 months).
No visa needed

UK booking agents/
tour operators: **Tailor Made Holidays**
5 Station Approach
Hinchley Wood
Surrey KT10 0SP
tel: (0208) 398 0188
fax: (0208) 398 6007
e-mail: chris@tailormadeholidays.co.uk

Lake Victoria and the River Nile at Murchison Falls, Uganda

Safari organizers   **Paul Goldring**
on the lake and   G & C Tours
to the falls: PO Box 619
Entebbe
Uganda
tel/fax: (256) 041321 479
mobile: (077) 502 155
and (077) 403 482
e-mail: gctours@imul.com

Airlines: Alliance Air (Heathrow–Entebbe)

Suggested
inoculations: Anti-malarial tablets, tetanus,
hepatitis A, diphtheria, yellow fever
(essential), typhoid, polio

Ugandan currency: 2500 Ugandan shillings to £1 sterling

Fishing licences: None required

Passport/visas: 10-year passport (valid 6 months).
Visa required, obtainable at Entebbe
Airport

INDEX

Italics indicate either illustrations or captions

Red River
Manitoba
Canada

Fraser River
British Columbia
Canada

Islamorada
Florida Keys
USA

The Bahamas

PACIFIC OCEAN

NORTH ATLAN